Healing with Shirdi Sai Baba

Nandini Dhanani

Healing with Shirdi Sai Baba
© 2021, Nandini Dhanani

All rights are reserved.
No part of this publication may be reproduced, stored in a retrieval system or transmitted, in any form or by any means, mechanical, photocopying, recording or otherwise, without prior written permission of the original publisher.

I bow down to Maa Kali, Lord Ganesh and Maa Saraswati and seek their blessings.

I bow down to my Sai, my Hiral Shah.

I bow down to my mother and father

Thank you Thank you Thank you.

**Communicated to Nandini Dhanani
in truth, humility and devotion**

I seek not joy nor sorrow
I seek not the stars or moon
All I wish is to bow at your feet
And be with You.
In Your smile, I see my self
In Your love, I find myself
You SAI are my Universe
I am but a shadow that follows You.

'If you take My name and remember Me
You will always find Me with you
If you call out to Me with love
You will find Me around you
If you sing to Me in devotion
You will find Me in your prayers
If you dance in joy and chant My name
You will find Me beside you
If you love Me like a mother
You will find My arms protecting you
If you give Me respect as a father
I will always be with you.'

Shirdi Sai Baba

'This is not just a book but Sai's blessing
It is not just a read but life lessons
Keep in mind that Sai is with you
And reading this book will bring you closer to Him.'

Baba Hiral Shah

'The reading of this book will help heal you,
Save you from mishaps and cure you of your illness
Read it with devotion and your dreams will come true.'
And reading this book will bring you closer to Him.'

Baba Hiral Shah

Contents

Preface *xiii*
Acknowledgements *xv*

1. **Sai Baba, Hiral Shah and I** **1**
2. **Messages from Sai** **5**
   At the feet of Sai 6
   A true Guru 9
   Spirituality 11
   Beliefs 12
   Choice to live 13
   Spread joy 14
   Karma 15
   Greed 17
   Seek forgiveness 18
   Cleanse yourself 19
   Don't condemn saints 20
   Consecrated Water 21
   Mother Earth 22
   Communicate 23
   Healers of Sai 24
3. **Sai Leelas** **25**
   Let love be your religion 26
   Egoistic Damodar 28
   Parth and Ragini 31
   Nanavali's desire for freedom 33
   Rajiv and his colleagues 35

Raman gives up on Sai	37
Navika's incomplete devotion	39
Listen to your Guru	40
Work or Family?	42
True love	44
Sai visits Jagdish's home	46
Whose cooking is better?	48
Dhanwanti and her family	50
Sai Baba saves Mahank	52
The man who abused	54
Mahendra in Kashi	56
Madhav and Rajshri	58
Tanushree reads the Satcharitra	60
Manvi and her mother	62
Peer pressure	64
Mahi and her new shoes	67
Lord Ganesha	69
Tahira and Sai	71
Saved by Sai	74
Dandekar and his family	76
Soumya's suffering	78
Zohaib comes to Mumbai	81
Satram	83
Kunti and Sai	85
Rain and storm	87
Faith can move mountains	89
Gayatri's deformity	92
Smriti and her friends	94
Aarti's spritual pride	96
Madhu visits the temple	98
4. Conversations with Sai	**101**
5. Pearls of Wisdom	**127**

6. Baba Hiral Shah and His Miracles	**143**
My Guru Baba Hiral Shah by Roshini Mahtani	145
Miracles of Sai Baba and Baba Hiral Shah	153
Stop Lying	154
Baba's love for his disciples	156
Duty first	158
Go back	160
Baba's refusal to Sarojini's choice	161
Chirag survives	162
You are what you eat	163
Guru is a shield	165
Humility	167
Baba blesses Tara and Mohan with a child	169

Preface

My Guru, Baba Hiral Shah had told me many years back that Sai would make me write a book, but I procrastinated. When I recently met a healer he spoke the same words that my Guru had told me years back, 'Sai will make you write a book.'

I did not know what I was meant to write, what would the format be like or what Sai would convey. I simply sat to write.

I invoked Him and the words began flowing. When Sai conveys His messages there is no Mind, there is no Me, the words just type itself on the computer and form sentences, paragraphs and pages. I did not even realize how I finished this book.

Sai is extremely generous and his love for his bhaktas is difficult to define. Many of Sai bhaktas will tell you that when he chooses you to write, he makes sure you are following his command.

It was my Guru Baba Hiral Shah who would ask me to write messages. Those messages would be from different saints and angels, but after he left his mortal body I stopped automatic writing. I thought why should I write? Who would validate? My Guru was not around, so how could I write? I was mistaken, for my Guru even after leaving his mortal body is around. My Guru is with Sai and he has made sure I fulfil the promise I made to him.

I humbly request Sai bhaktas to accept this gift from Sai. Read it daily and keep it in your shrine, for these are his words that have been inked forever. Words that will heal those that suffer. Sai is always looking out for his children. When he puts his hand on your head, your problems disappear. The voltage of your suffering lessens.

My Guru and my Sai have been my anchor and my guide. I am grateful for all the comforts that Sai has provided me with in my life and has given me an opportunity to serve him. I consider myself mere dust at his feet.

I request you to please read this book with utmost devotion, for each and every word in this book is spoken by Sai. Immerse yourself in this gift of love from Sai. I am but a mere instrument conveying his messages. No special powers are required to communicate with Shirdi Sai Baba and it is his mercy and command that I have followed.

It is in the reading of books on Sai, his messages and his conversations that one is enlightened on many subjects. If your love for Sai is immense then he will communicate directly or through his healers, who can guide you. To be in constant touch with Him it is not necessary to sit in prayers for hours but instead invoke Him and seek His guidance. Whenever you are in distress or looking for solutions reach out to him.

I bow at Sai's feet. With folded hands I seek His guidance and direction.

Acknowledgements

I have been a devout follower of Sai and it was with his blessings that I met my Guru, Baba Hiral Shah. Baba Hiral Shah was a pure soul, who dedicated his life to the betterment of humanity. I thank my Sai and my Baba Hiral Shah for their unconditional love and am forever grateful to them for choosing me as their instrument to write this book for the benefit of humanity.

When one wishes to walk the path of spirituality, life throws hurdles to deviate the soul from the path. I have faced many obstacles in my quest for spirituality and am still learning and evolving. I stumbled and fell many a times and gave up on spirituality; but I am for ever indebted to my Guru and Sai, who never gave up on me.

I am grateful to my maternal and paternal grandparents for their blessings. My parents Sushila and Narain Sawlani, for their unconditional love.

Manjhand Durbar in Khar, Mumbai has been the eternal abode of my grandparents where they volunteered to serve on all holy days. The present Mahant Swami Mohandasji is one of the purest souls on this earth and his divine eyes speak a thousand words. I would like to thank Swami Mohandasji, for his unconditional love towards all.

I thank all Sai bhakts with whom I share my experiences and love for Sai. Especially my sister Roshini Mahtani who has been a guide for all the followers of Baba Hiral Shah after he left his mortal body. Roshini is a role model disciple and communicates with Sai and has written many holy books. These holy books are placed in the shrine of

Lakshmi Narayan Temple in Khar Mumbai. I am grateful to her for sharing the experiences of Baba's devotees and penning her feelings for Baba. I extend my gratitude to my brother-in-law Mahesh (Manna) Mahtani who is an inspiration in selfless love and dedication towards Sai. Mahesh and Roshini's dedication and discipline in looking after Sai aasthan's across the globe is praise worthy.

I thank my husband Lal and children Sanam, Sahil and Armaan. My mentor Sandeep Adnani for his consistent support and guidance, my extended family and Sai Parivar for their unconditional love. Sai Parivar all around the world is bonded by their love and devotion for Sai Baba and Baba Hiral Shah. We are forever indebted to our Guru for teaching us the right values and training us to live a disciplined and devotional life.

Sai Baba, Hiral Shah and I

Sai Baba is always with us. All we need to do is connect to his energy. Some are comfortable singing devotional songs, some meditating and some undergo severe penance. Each path leads to the same, Sai. The difference lies in the network. Each one chooses the network that resonates with them.

The simplest and easiest way to pray is by talking to Sai. Communicate with him throughout the day. Be mindful of his presence. Believe that he is there, for he is in you, around you. Your mind distracts you from reality and the only way to be aware of the Truth is by communicating with Sai.

We have within us two voices that are used for communication. One voice communicates with the Truth and the other with Darkness. The dark voice keeps us away from the Truth. It thrives on our lethargy, greed, anger, pride and jealousy.

In the world of social media, we are communicating constantly with our loved ones, our friends, relations and others. But we are unable to communicate with our higher soul. Our higher soul that is in tune with Sai Baba. Shut your mind out from the world and talk to him. Believe that he is there listening to you, allow the doors of communication to remain open.

It was my Master Baba Hiral Shah who I had observed communicating with all deities. He bowed at dargahs and temples, to Ram and Rahim, to Mother Mary and Guru

Nanak. He would place his hand on my hand and with his blessings I would write. He would say today this saint or deity will communicate and I would sit with my pen and paper and messages would flow. I never paused to think even for a second. This book too is written with the blessings of Sai, through different Angels and Masters.

Earlier, I would never take automatic writing seriously. I knew it was not me writing, for whenever I thought it was me, the flow would stop itself and I then struggled to pen the words. This was enough evidence that there was an energy that made me write. Baba never gave up on me, but I did mentally, although not subconsciously. My Guru once said to me, 'Every birth you have deviated from the path.'

'Not in this birth Baba,' I had promised. Did I keep the promise? After my Guru's demise, I did sway away for a while as I felt abandoned after he left his mortal body. Sai watched, Baba watched, and Baba Ashraf my Hiral Shah's guru watched me and let me be. Till I realized that there was no one like my SAIHIRA.

Everyone needs a direction and I had lost mine after the passing away of my Master, but Sai has his ways of bringing lost souls back to him. He loves his devotees, even if they move away from the path. And Sai did the same with me. Although I did love Sai but there came a time when I stopped thinking and focussed only on gaining knowledge through books. But it did not help, for I could not recollect even a few lines from the scriptures that I read.

Life throws many obstacles in our path and it is our will power and faith that helps us cross these hurdles. When we are the most broken is when we need to have the maximum faith in Sai. At that moment surrendering at his feet is vital.

Offer a leaf to him, he is happy.
Offer your vices to him, he will take them.
Offer your love to him, he will return hundred-fold.
His grace will help you in every decision of your life.

Baba Hiral Shah

Sai Aasthan in Torremolinos, Spain

Shirdi Sai Baba

Messages from Sai

At the feet of Sai

At Sai's feet there is abundance. The joy that we search outside is within us. But due to our busy lives we never dwell within. This pandemic is a forewarning, a teaching that humans need to slow down. It is time to dive deep within and find happiness that you so desperately look for outside. Many a life have been lost in this pandemic and many families did not get a chance to see their loved ones as they suffered. This pandemic is a reminder that life is unpredictable and short. It is a reminder that when one leaves the mortal body, they are alone. As humans stayed indoors during their lockdowns, birds and beasts roamed freely. Oceans were cleansed, the air was purer and Mother Earth felt lighter.

Nature was gifted to humans in a pristine form. Humans have destroyed Nature and this is but a warning from Nature to mend their ways. Enough time was given to each and every human being to dive within and contemplate.

If your Higher self has reminded you of your goal, work towards it now. If your Higher self has taught you that you need to slow down, then slow down. If it has taught you to serve others, serve. This pandemic is nothing but an opportunity to evolve. It is time for self-love, self- realization, self -connection. It is time to tune in to the network that is open for connection to Sai, to your Master and through them to the Supreme Power. Whatever your goal, work towards it. Nothing is achieved by procrastinating.

Change for the better, grow as a human being. Be kind to all. Think positive thoughts and you will attain higher status in the spiritual world. What is this spiritual world like? This world is full of angels and saints and good souls. The spiritual world has many realms and your vibrations will lead you to your realm. If you do good to others, good will happen to you. Stop condemning, hating, politicizing and throwing muck at others.

Alarm bells are ringing, don't snooze it. Wake up. It is the grace of the Masters and Saints who have prayed for peace and calm on earth, thank them as they have been instrumental in saving humankind. It is time for gratitude not attitude. It is this pandemic that has allowed a lot of dirt to surface. Simple measure of hygiene is the only cure for this problem. Similarly, life questions are easy and simple to answer. Life is not as complicated as we have made it out to be.

Life is joyful, live it.
Life is a gift, accept it.
Life is a journey, walk it.

'*In your journey you will come across many a saint, teachers and those that will be in direct connection with Me. Recognize them and they will guide you towards Me,*' Sai Baba

Readers, please think of Sai Baba and his grace upon yourself as you read the experiences of devotees and Sai's poems and messages. In many a form and many a ways Sai projects himself in his writings.

Cleanse yourself with his stories, his leelas. Let your emotions flow. These experiences will help you wash away your misery.

Blessings from above flow easily on those who have faith in Sai. Faith can move mountains and prayers go a long way. Some sit for hours in meditation yet the moment they get up from their meditation they are unkind to people around them. Your life should be meditative and calm. It may take years but one has to work towards it.

Only when you draw yourself closer to Sai will you begin to see the changes within. Prayer, meditation, compassion and devotion should be a consistent part of your day. Don't wake up one morning and expect that because you meditated the whole day prior you are now an expert.

Even sages take years to achieve that stillness of mind and body. Open the doors of communication to Sai, speak to him and above all listen to him. If you want to share some news, do it with Sai. Do not think that he is not listening, he is and don't be surprised if he responds.

Sai enjoys some good fun too. He wants you to treat him as your own. Once you start talking to him, devotion will follow. He will become your personal trainer and guide you through the darkness and lead you to Light.

Surrender at his feet,
For at his feet you will find peace,
Peace that will lead you to Light,
Through thick and thin.
Sai will be with you,
If you hold his hand once,
Never will Sai ever leave you.

A true Guru

Things don't always work out the way you want them to, during those times you look for refuge and guidance. You search for a ray of hope. A hope to survive, to grow, to evolve, to come out of a situation.

It is the role of a Guru to help you out in situations where you lose hope. It is your Guru, who holds your hand and guides you through. Never under estimate the power of a True Guru.

It is your Guru who helps you cross the turbulences and problems that life throws at you. Your Guru will never let you down. Not for money nor fame will he address your pain, it is his longing and love for human kind, that he guides souls. One who has merged with the True light, can make your path easier to travel.

Don't feel disheartened if you have not found a Guru in physical form, for if you call out to Sai, with a true heart and longing, Sai will accept you as his own. Sai is a Sadhguru. Once you are under his protection, he will become your Guru, your mother, father, brother, sister and friend. With Sai you can share every detail of your life.

Bow to Sai, there is no one like him. He doesn't need to be in a physical form to talk to you. He doesn't need a form to guide you. It is in remembering him that you will hear him. That day is not too far when every soul will experience him within.

*Think not what the world can give you,
think what you can do for the world.*

*Think not what Sai can do for you,
think what are you doing for Sai.*

What does Sai want?

Love and devotion.

What does Sai expect?

Only compassion.

What does Sai wish?

That you are filled with good values.

What does Sai believe?

*That one day you will do what he wishes for you to do
and that you will break free from the veil of
illusion and find the Truth.*

If SAI believes in you, why don't you?

Believe, believe, believe… that Sai is here with you.

Spirituality

Spirituality is the key to happiness. Work towards evolving your soul. You waste a lot of time watching content that is of no significance to your soul. Instead, if you dedicated your time to reading scriptures, watching Nature and listening to stories of deities, you will find inner peace. That inner stability will lead you towards self-realization.

When you watch violent content, you are flooding your mind with negative thoughts. You are gripped by negativity, which is darkness. Keep a balance in your life. Do not over watch anything that fills your mind with negative thoughts, thoughts that will keep you away from your goal. Your goal is not just to drink, eat, sleep and entertain yourself. Your soul has a purpose on this earth and you need to work towards it.

Don't unwind at nights with negative visuals. Instead spend time in silence or watch anything that will nurture your soul. If each human being works on themselves, they will be stronger emotionally, physically, mentally and spiritually.

Life without prayers,
is like a boat without rudders,
a bird without feathers,
an ocean without waves.

Beliefs

In this world there are all kinds of people. Some who believe in the Supreme Power, some who pendulate and others who are in disagreement to the existence of God. Every human has a right to their thought, for God has given humans a brain that directs them. A mind that leads their thoughts and intellect that helps them distinguish. Yet many are of the belief that there is no God.

Sai asks of those learned men, if the Universe was created by 'The big bang theory,' then how is it that each species is different. Each human is different. How is it that despite being different externally everyone's internal organs function in the same way? Even when you perform an experiment in a lab you need a scientist behind who initiates the experiment. It does not happen on its own. The Sun, the Moon, the stars the planets are not an outcome of a big bang. The Supreme Power has lovingly created this Universe. Your intellect is nothing compared to his vastness. You cannot judge the Creator as you are incapable of understanding His greatness.

But those who believe in Him and walk the path of spirituality, within them is the desire to know the Supreme Power and are initiated into seeing this reality. It is those seekers who have crushed their ego, let go off their intellect and surrendered to His feet that experience true joy. Those who don't believe in the Supreme Power are stuck in the mundane detail of life, they are content with material possessions and reaching the Moon. If you wish to come out of this cycle of life and birth then the only way is to work towards Self-realization.

Choice to live

It is your choice, how you wish to live your life. Happy or sad. Strong or weak, joyous or sorrowful. God gives you choices, it is your decision to live your life the way you wish to.

If you accept pain, your suffering will turn to joy. If you complain, your suffering will be double fold. You are the decision maker of your life.

It may not be easy to live life joyously when suffering. But with love and devotion every suffering becomes trivial. It is through prayers and guidance of a Guru, that you can learn the art of detaching yourself from your suffering and accepting whatever comes your way.

Another day, another night,
Another life, another death.

Life keeps moving,
Why look behind?

Keep moving ahead,
And work on yourself.

Through your journeys keep evolving,
Keep spreading joy and laughter.

Spread joy

Joy is contagious, but if you are unhappy from within how will you spread joy. Evolving in spirituality will help you reach that state of ecstasy.

Inner growth is attained by disciplining oneself and rising early morning is one of the habits that devotees must establish in their life. Rise with the sun and you will need no kind of intoxication. Sunlight has the power to fill your soul with joy.

Communicating with Sai will fill you with positivity. In loving Sai and bowing to his will is joy. Loving him unconditionally is joy. Your presence will be a blessing to those who come in contact with you. Your words will heal those hearts that are filled with sorrow.

Do good to others and spread joy, for the more you give the more you get. When you spread joy to others, you will enhance your karma.

Light up a room with your laughter,
Light up the Universe with your goodness,
Walk the path of truth and surrender to Sai.

You will find peace within,
An effulgent light will you be,
An asset to human kind.

Karma

Thoughts, words and actions determine one's karma. It is births and births of karmic accounts that come into play. Whatever you go through in this birth is a result of prior births, so when you are unwell or suffering from a disease do not think that I did nothing. For if you did nothing you would not be on this earth.

Each soul has a prior karmic account that needs to be cleared. Through charity, service, kind acts and other good ways you can increase the account of your good actions. When the balance is higher of your good, your suffering weakens in intensity.

It is with good thoughts, words and actions your suffering can be diminished. But if your account is fully negative, then it's time to work very hard to balance it with good deeds. Begin by thinking good for others, discard your pride and greed. When you have changed your thinking your words and actions too will be sattvic.

Sai asks of his devotees to walk the right path. In many a ways Sai has shown us through example how he served the needy and poor. Along with service he taught devotion. Life is precious don't waste it, instead work on yourself. Focus on things that will help you evolve.

Sai asks of his children not to waste their time running after fame, wealth and success. Instead He asks to look within and find the true purpose of life.

"One has to reap what one sows and there is no escape unless one suffers and squares up one's old debts and dealings with others" - Chapter 47 of Sai Satcharitra.

When time comes to leave this Earth,
What is that you will take?

What is it that you will leave?

Ask yourself these questions everyday,
And you will find the answers within.

Those answers that will bring a change in you,
The change that Sai awaits.

Greed

Of all the vices in the world the most prevalent during these times is greed. Greed to acquire wealth, greed for power, greed for material gains, greed for intoxication and greed for success and fame. Greed, that has crossed its limits.

Intoxicated by greed, humans have forgotten the true purpose of their life and are stooping to the lowest level to fulfil this vice.

The Universe is imbalanced due to the extreme greed amongst humans. This greed if not controlled will lead to further calamities. Every human has to control their greed by changing their thinking, their lifestyle and their attitude.

The riches you have accumulated will not be of any use when disaster strikes. Time is precious and is slipping from your hands. Time that will never come back.

When each one brings a change within, the world too will change. Work on yourself, without wasting more time. For a better world tomorrow, control your greed today.

Be the change, be the hope for human kind,
Let not your desires blanket you,
Let not greed destroy you.

Control your ego before it controls you,
Change within and respect human life.

Seek forgiveness

The world is going through a major shift. A shift that will take many lives and will destroy the ego of humans. Those that are filled with hunger for power and greed, those that take pride in their material gains, those that believe they have conquered the world. It is time to ask for forgiveness from the Supreme.

Forgiveness for the inhumane behaviour, forgiveness for the irrational abuse of Nature. Forgiveness for pride and forgiveness for being insensitive towards animals and birds.

Seek forgiveness through prayer, 'I have been insensitive and uncaring towards the gifts I have received. I have harmed and destroyed the earth for my greed. I seek your forgiveness and bow at your feet.'

Don't wait for judgement day to seek forgiveness,
Pray today, for Time waits for no one,
Fall at His feet and surrender.

Cleanse yourself

When Sai ask's you to do something, it is only for your benefit. It is for your growth. Sai wishes to see each of his child find inner peace.

Each soul is divine and needs to clear the cobwebs that have accumulated through births. Now is the opportunity. There is no severe penance required but chanting his name and doing good to others.

As you cleanse your body with soap and water, cleanse your soul with goodness and charity.

Keep your values intact,
Don't get carried away.

The sparkling gems are an illusion,
They will lead you away,
Away from your goal,
Away from Sai.

Don't condemn saints

After many births of penance, a saint is born. Saints who take birth to shake humans from their deep slumber.

These are saints who have experienced TRUTH and come on this Earth to help those lost souls who are incapable of finding the path to liberation.

Don't condemn saints or make fun of them. You are not aware of their power, so do not think them less. Simplicity and humility are the two gems of these saints. They take avatars of normal beings to guide and protect others.

If you don't agree to the teachings of certain saints, don't follow them. But don't make the blunder of ridiculing them. Condemning saints will only add to your negative karmas.

A guru will guide you,
Guru will hold your hand and lead you,
From darkness to light.

Consecrated Water

Water is a component that is made of hydrogen and oxygen and has memory. Thus it is important that one drinks pure water. To make sure you are drinking water that is not contaminated with negativity, energise it with good thoughts and feelings.

Keep water in a copper vessel or glass beside you whenever you sit to pray, chant or meditate.

Drinking that energised water is highly beneficial and sprinkling this water around your home will help eliminate negativity. If you feel your house is being attacked by negativity read the Gayatri Mantra and sprinkle the energised water. For ill health chant Maha Mrityunjaya Mantra and sprinkle the consecrated water on the person who is unwell.

Consecrated water has the power to heal.

Water is the source of life,
Water is a form of the divine,
Consecrated water will protect you from evil.

Mother Earth

It is the prayers and blessings of Saints and Masters that has saved humanity from the wrath of Mother Earth. It is their prayers and guidance that is saving human kind from falling further.

Fire, killings, pollution have been on the rise, the consequences of which humans are now experiencing. Beasts, birds and humans all have the right to live in peace. But humans have taken undue advantage of their intelligence and destroyed Mother Earth for their selfish reasons.

Respect Nature. It is time to stop wastage, it is time to bring a change and stop destruction. Seek forgiveness from Mother Earth.

Let there be peace,
Let there be love,
Do away with your greed,
And respect Mother Earth.

Communicate

Take time out to write what the universe wishes to convey. Connect to your Higher self through writing. Sit in silence and pen your thoughts.

When you shut your eyes and remember Him, you connect to your Higher Self. Messages from the Universe flow through you. Ask of Sai for his grace and you will find words flowing easily.

Ask Sai to make you his instrument,
Bow to your Master for guidance,
Let the words flow on paper,
At first what you scribble will make no sense,
But slowly the writing,
will turn out to be words of wisdom.

Healers of Sai

Let not your mind be in doubt when it comes to these simple human beings who come across as householders. Many healers have been blessed by Sai with power to heal.

Sai's mission is to help those who are lost in this journey of life. Healers of Sai have taken upon themselves to guide the souls back Home. Healers are striving hard to comply with their Sai's wishes. They have dedicated their life to the betterment of humanity. These healers have taken upon themselves to guide mankind and free it from the shackles of greed, lust, desire, anger and hatred.

The road to Sai is not difficult,
Nor is it difficult to find him,
It is your mind that is veiled by Maya,
That complicates things,
Shed your illusions by chanting Sai.

SAI LEELAS

In the following pages are the experiences of the devotees of Baba.

Through these Leelas, Baba has conveyed various lessons

Let love be your religion

Shalini loved Asif but she feared telling her parents about him, for she knew they would never accept a boy from another faith.

Manju and Suresh were on the look-out for a good Hindu boy for their only daughter Shalini but had not been successful. On a neighbour's suggestion to visit Shirdi and seek Baba's blessings for Shalini, the family set out from their village.

The family took a bullock cart from their village but before they could reach the next village, their bullock cart collided with a truck and Shalini flew off the cart. She hit her head against a tree. Manju and Suresh suffered a few injuries. Shalini lay unconscious and badly bruised and was rushed to a hospital. Shalini was immediately operated upon.

Asif reached the hospital as soon as he heard about Shalini's accident and cried as he saw his love lay semiconscious in the ICU. Manju and Suresh asked Asif to leave when they heard of his relation with Shalini. Asif pleaded to be around but Manju and Suresh were livid to know of their daughter's love life.

A shattered Asif then took a bus and left for Shirdi, to seek blessings from Sai. Asif stayed in Shirdi for a few days and visited the Samadhi Mandir everyday and then would sit outside Dwarkamai. On the fourth day when Asif stepped out of the Samadhi Mandir, a young man walked up to him.

The saffron robed man told Asif, *'Allah maalik karenge woh theek ho jaegi. Ab accha hi hoga* (Allah maalik will bless her and she will be fine. Now only good will happen) and asked him to go back to Shalini. He asked him not to forget to take the Udi and apply on her.

Asif bowed his head and thanked the bearded man and left from Shirdi. Asif went straight to the hospital. Shalini had been shifted to the ward and lay semi-conscious due to the heavy medications. Asif requested Manju to let him apply the udi, that he had brought from Shirdi.

Manju gave in to Asif's pleas and let him smear Shalini with Sai's udi. Manju watched Asif sit beside Shalini and chant the name of Sai. After a while Shalini opened her eyes and on seeing Asif, she wept with joy.

In two weeks Shalini had recuperated and Asif went back to Shirdi to thank Sai. The saint who had told him all would be fine, stood beside a pole with a begging bowl in his hand.

Asif fell at his feet and kept a five hundred rupee note in his bowl. The saint laughed and commented, *'waqt guzar gaya na?(bad times have passed right?) She was not meant to be on this earth plane. But she did due to your devotion. You passed your test and your love won.'* On hearing the saint's words, Asif wept bitterly. How could he have not recognised his Sai? 'You will soon be a groom,' said Sai. Asif unable to control his joy asked Sai to wait while he got him some tea and snacks. But when he returned Sai had disappeared.

A few months later Asif and Shalini were married and visited Shirdi every month to thank their Sai who had made the impossible, possible.

MORAL: The barriers of religion are man-made. It does not matter who you worship, what matters is how true is your love.

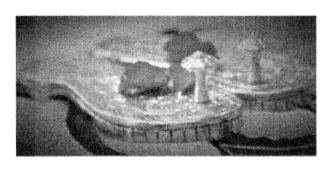

Egoistic Damodar

Damodar was a strict disciplinarian and followed his religious practices diligently. He was a Brahmin by birth who spent most of his time praying. His wife Sujata was an ardent devotee of Sai, but did not follow any ritualistic practices. All she did was chant the name of Sai through out the day.

Damodar ridiculed his wife for not praying, the way he did. He woke up early in the morning and invoked all the deities and read scriptures. Sujata would organize and keep everything ready for Damodar for his ritualistic prayers, but even if one item from the paraphernalia went missing, Damodar would shout at his wife.

Sujata on the other hand started her day with a smile, she bowed to the sun, expressed her gratitude to Mother Earth and Nature, fed animals and birds and conversed with Sai. She was forever grateful to Sai for her health and family. At the age of sixty-five, she would clean and scrub the floors, prepare meals and keep in touch with her two married daughters who lived abroad. When their families visited Delhi, they would enjoy themselves and spend time laughing. But Damodar would never take time out for his children as his rituals took up most of his time.

Damodar would tease his wife that she would never attain liberation. He humiliated her for not being detached from worldly affairs. But Sujata never flinched or responded to her husband's ill remarks about her spirituality. In her heart she knew that all she desired was to serve Sai.

Sujata's daughters were keen that their mother keep a helper and not work so hard at that age. But Sujata refused for she was contented and enjoyed running her home. She was against anyone bringing in a different energy to their home and kept her space pure. Her daughters found their mother's obsession with her home incomprehensible.

One day as Sujata was talking to her Sai, He told her that it was time she kept a helper to assist her. Sujata never refuted her Sai's command. It so happened that within a few days of hiring a helper, Damodar had a severe heart attack and was operated upon. Sujata was grateful to Sai. As the helper attended to the household chores, she could give time to her husband.

Their daughters flew down for a while to see to their ailing father and were impressed the way their mother continued looking after her husband's needs. They applauded her patience and dedication towards her husband. They watched their mother serve unconditionally. She tended to her husband's needs and did not appoint any nurse.

Time went by, Damodar recovered from his weakness and their daughters left for their homes. Damodar began spending hours at the temple and continued reprimanding his wife for every little thing, but Sujata stayed calm.

One day as Damodar sat in the temple preparing for his morning prayers, Sujata requested her husband to let her visit Shirdi. She asked Damodar to join in or give her permission to go for a few days. Damodar who was preparing the aarti thali flung it towards Sujata and abused her for not caring about her duties.

Sujata did not react to her husband's anger. With tears in her eyes she quietly picked up the thali, washed it and handed it back to her husband. Damodar lit the aarti and prayed. Sujata sat quietly, her eyes brimming with tears as her husband sang the evening aarti.

That night Sai came to Damodar in his dream. He asked Damodar to recite one of the verses from the Bhagavad Gita. Damodar recited a few lines in his dream. Sai asked him the meaning and Damodar explained them. Sai then questioned Damodar if he practised what he read? Had he been able to control his vices? Damodar had no response as the scene where he flung the aarti thali played innumerable times in front of him.

Sai then told Damodar that his prayers had no meaning. If one did not treat their own with love and respect then how did they expect to be accepted by God. Damodar felt his body crumble and he woke up sweating.

Damodar rushed towards the temple where his wife was organizing the paraphernalia for his morning prayers. He fell at Sujata's feet and asked for forgiveness and told her that they will go to Shirdi.

MORAL: Mechanical prayers and recitations are not enough to attain God. One has to love and respect those around them.

Let it go, whatever bothers you,
Let it go, of what others think of you,
Surrender yourself at the feet of Sai,
And you will find happiness forever.

Care not what they say,
Care not what they think,
If your conscience is clear,
Nothing can take your peace away.

Parth and Ragini

Ragini prayed to Sai everyday for her husband's success. A few years after their marriage him business began flourishing. Ragini was ever grateful to her Sai. But Parth believed it was his intellect that brought him wealth.

Parth's growing business and success attracted many new friends into his life who were using Parth for personal gains. Parth was carried away by the attention and began advising his friends on how to run a successful business. Parth's ego had been inflated by his friends. Friends who were now influencing him into drinking, gambling and womanizing.

Ragini was aware of her husband's wrong company and tried hard to guide him. But Parth would not listen to his wife nor parents. Parth believed he was doing nothing wrong.

Ragini wept in front of Sai and prayed to him for his blessings. Years passed but she saw no change in her husband. Parth never took time out for his children.

Parth's parents refrained from telling their son anything. They did not want to lose out on the financial gains from their son. Ragini was saddened that Sai was not answering her prayers but she did not give up hope.

In a dream Sai revealed to Ragini that in her previous birth she had been ruthless to Parth and thus was facing these issues. Sai promised her that soon she would be relieved of her past karmas. Ragini accepted her fate and continued praying to Sai, visiting his temple everyday and attending kirtans.

After a few years, Parth's business began seeing a downfall. Parth had been cheated by his business associates and lost a lot of money. Unable to face the losses Parth fell sick, a depressed Parth was unable to get himself to work. Ragini did not give up on her husband nor his business. With time the business had recovered the losses and Parth's health too had improved.

Parth apologized to his wife and children and one night was blessed by Sai in his dream.

MORAL: A man should treat his wife with respect and love, similarly a woman too should be by her husband in his difficult times. If any one of them move away from their path they should remind each other of the vows they had made to each other. Love is the only way to win each other. Anger and hatred only create distance. With love you can melt mountains.

Human relations are bounded by karmas. It is your karmas that bring certain situations in your life but it is upto you how you react in those situations. It is upto you to face your problems or run away from them.

Nanavali's desire for freedom

Nanavali, a bhakta of Sai felt burdened by his family and their demands. He would cry at the feet of Sai for freedom from responsibilities and social pressures. He desired to live by himself and spend time in devotion. His daughter had dreams of completing her higher education for which she required funds and his wife loved hosting people in their home and traveling. Burdened all the time with financial pressure, Nanavali felt suffocated with life. His frustration had converted into anger and he began detesting his family. He prayed to Sai to please allow him to become a monk.

In his dream, one-night Nanavali sat below a tree, meditating on Sai. He tried hard to meditate but the sound of animals and the rustling of branches and leaves disturbed him. As he was meditating, Nanavali sensed a large animal running towards him. Nanavali opened his eyes and saw a lion approaching him. Nanavali cried out to Sai to save him.

'But wasn't this what you wanted? To meditate in the forest, away from your family responsibilities?' Sai's voice reverberated in the jungle.

Nanavali asked Sai to please come in his form and save him. 'Sai please save me. I want to attain liberation not death,' Nanavali pleaded to Sai, his eyes staring at the fierce animal drawing closer.

'You don't need to run away from home, to attain liberation Nanavali. You can attain God by complying with your duties. You can attain God by spreading love and joy. You can attain God by helping those in need. Running away from your responsibilities will not bring you closer to God,' Sai appeared in front of Nanavali.

The lion was now sitting at the feet of Sai. Nanavali's body tensed as he saw the animal close to him.

Nanavali pleaded to Sai to make the animal disappear and to take him back home. Next instant Nanavali disappeared from the jungle and woke up sweating. Seeing his wife beside him Nanavali breathed a sigh of relief. He thanked Sai for his guidance.

Then onwards Nanavali performed his duties with love. After their daughter's marriage Nanavali's wife too passed away. Nanavali then left for Shirdi and stayed there serving in the temple.

MORAL: One cannot find Sai by running away from their duties. Being in this world and chanting the name of the Lord brings us closer to Sai.

It is in prayers you will find Me,
It is in silence you will hear Me,
It is in Nature you will see Me,
It is in kindness you will sense Me,
Lift the veil of ignorance,
And recognize the divinity around and within you.

Rajiv and his colleagues

Rajiv worked diligently in his office and kept away from office gossip. He was liked by his boss, his manager and many of his colleagues for his easy-going nature. Except for a few colleagues who despised his popularity, others were all fond of Rajiv.

These four colleagues who were fearful that Rajiv would be promoted, conjured a plan to defame him. Each of the colleague went up to their manager Mahesh and on some pretext spread wrong stories about Rajiv. Slowly there were rumours about Rajiv bad mouthing Mahesh to the office staff. Mahesh was furious to hear about Rajiv's sly remarks and changed his attitude towards Rajiv.

Rajiv was taken aback by Mahesh's changed behaviour and told his wife Kanti about it. Kanti who was a devotee of Sai, listened patiently to her husband. Kanti knew how naive her husband was and how it was impossible for him to bad mouth anyone.

Kanti who was a devout Sai follower communicated to Sai her husband's problem and Sai responded to her query the following day and asked her to tell Rajiv to talk to his manager Mahesh and clear the air. Sai informed Kanti that there were four colleagues at the office who were envious of Rajiv's success.

Rajiv, a simple man was not even aware that there was anyone like this in office but when Kanti told him that it was a message from Sai, he agreed to talk to Mahesh. Bowing his head in reverence to Sai, Rajiv went to the office and met Mahesh. At first Mahesh ignored Rajiv's request of talking to him personally. But through the day when Rajiv kept persisting Mahesh let him speak. Rajiv with folded hands told Mahesh what Sai had told his wife. Mahesh then asked Rajiv a few questions to understand the truth. After twenty minutes into the conversation, Mahesh realized how foolish he had been to be carried away by frivolous gossip.

Mahesh called those four colleagues again and asked them questions about Rajiv. This time Mahesh could see through their jealousy and understood that they had been lying to him.

Meanwhile Rajiv and Kanti read the Satcharitra and pleaded to Sai to save Rajiv from the web of lies his colleagues had created in the office. After few weeks Rajiv was called to Mahesh's cabin. Mahesh announced to Rajiv that he had been promoted.

It was Sai's grace that Rajiv had been saved from the malicious intention of his colleagues.

MORAL: Rajiv chose not to retaliate to the gossip and slandering of his colleagues. Instead he prayed to Sai for guidance. No harm can come to those who are pure at heart.

Raman gives up on Sai

Raman was devoted to Sai and worshipped him devoutly till he met his wife Sandhya.

After his marriage, Raman had no time for prayers. Sandhya too was not in favour of idol worship. She would nag Raman for his belief in Sai.

Raman gave up on his prayers and got engrossed in his duties. Sandhya introduced him to her friends. Friends who were attached to their vices and taught Raman to smoke, drink and gamble. Raman was carried away by the lure of a glamorous fun filled life.

After two years of marriage Raman and Sandhya were blessed with a son, Rahul. Rahul since the age of five years would stand by the altar and gaze at the idol of Sai. He had seen his father bow his head by the altar and Rahul would do the same.

Raman on the other hand had become addicted to gambling and drinking and was spending less time at home. Sandhya at times regretted introducing Raman to her friends and keeping him away from his beliefs.

When Rahul was to turn eight years, Sandhya asked her son what he would like for his birthday. Rahul asked his mother to take him to Shirdi. Sandhya was surprised to hear her son talk about Shirdi. The last time they had visited Shirdi was when Raman and she got married. It was Sandhya who had pulled Raman away from Sai and that guilt had been gnawing at her.

Sandhya was sorry that she nagged Raman and distanced him from his Sai. But Sai never left Raman. Sandhya conveyed to Raman, the desire of their son to visit Shirdi. At first Raman disagreed but on Rahul's insistence they went to Shirdi.

When Raman stood in front of the Samadhi Mandir he saw Baba sitting with his arms wide open and smiling at him. Raman bowed at the feet of Sai and asked for his forgiveness and promised Sai that he would never deviate from his path.

Through Rahul, Sai had reminded Raman of his true Nature. After that day Raman changed his ways and left drinking, smoking and gambling.

MORAL: At times Sai talks to you through others. Listen to Him for He is always protecting you. You may distance yourself from Him, but He is always protecting you.

At the feet of Sai, let go off your anger,
At his doorstep, drop all your desires,
Knock at his door not to gain, but give,
Surrender at his threshold, your ego and sins,
When you have bowed at his feet and surrendered,
You will not have to worry about your future.

Navika's incomplete devotion

Navika meditated and worshipped Sai with devotion. But her calmness would disappear the moment she stepped out of the small temple in her home.

Navika's samskaras from her earlier birth were of anger and envy. Her vices would force her to react to every situation heatedly. She was envious of friends and family. Navika would be angry with her husband if he went out with his friends.

One night, Sai appeared in Navika's dream and asked her to forego of her anger or she would suffer. Navika promised Sai in her dream that she would change and was calm for two days. On the third day when her husband returned late from work she fought with him. This time the fight led to Navika having a stroke. Her left side was paralysed due to the attack. Navika was forewarned but did not obey her Sai's command.

Navika's family looked after her with love. Her husband spent time with her and her children were constantly around her. Navika felt ashamed of herself and prayed to Sai for his forgiveness.

After a few months of therapy and treatment Navika was slightly better and was able to move her arm and leg. Grateful to her Sai, Navika changed her behaviour. With time she learned to control her anger and her irritation. She was kind to her husband and patient with her children. In a year's time Navika was back to her normal self.

MORAL: Accept your flaws and work on them. Don't let your negativity destroy your health and home.

Listen to your Guru

Shanti was a stubborn woman and spoke harshly to all. She criticised, condemned and at times demeaned people around her. Proud of herself and her beauty, Shanti ridiculed those who didn't look after their well-being.

Her husband Raja was a kind man who loved his wife immensely and overlooked her flaws. He was an ardent devotee of Sai and kept himself engrossed. Shanti would insult her daughter-in-law and treat her poorly but her son did not have the courage to tell his mother that she was wrong. Everyone at home feared Shanti's anger and harsh words.

Their Guru who was aware of Shanti's core nature advised her to change herself. He instructed her to control her thoughts, words and actions. But Shanti would disregard her Guru's words and believe that the disciples around him, were filling his ears. Believing herself to be right, she stopped visiting her Guru and began condemning him.

After her husband Raja's death things changed at home. Shanti could no longer control her son and daughter-in-law. Her son had taken over the financial matters and her daughter-in-law took charge of their home. Shanti was not allowed to involve herself in any decisions and was kept away from her grand-children. Shanti had no friends either and spent her time all by herself in her room. After a couple of years, Shanti was shifted to a nursing home due to her mental illness.

Some devotees are too egoistic and are not ready to accept their flaws. Not realizing that when a Guru guides his disciple, it is for their benefit.

MORAL: Your present actions affect your future. What you sow, so shall you reap.

Think not what to give Me,
It is your love filled heart,
that pleases ME for ever.

When you give to the needy,
It comes back to you ten-fold.

What you rob from someone,
you pay back hundred-fold.

Think and act on whatever you do.

Your actions of today will,
Determine your future.

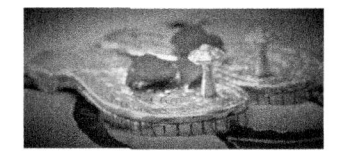

Work or Family?

Rashmi worked and lived in Mumbai. Her parents and brother lived in Nashik. Her boyfriend Raj stayed with her in her apartment on the weekends.

Rashmi did not get along too well with her parents and rarely visited them. She disagreed with their belief system and was against idol worship. Her parents had a large idol of Sai in their home but Rashmi never found it necessary to bow at his feet. Rashmi's younger brother Angad would plead her to visit them, but she would prefer being in Mumbai and enjoying herself.

One day when Rashmi was returning from work, her car broke down. She tried calling her boyfriend Raj but he did not answer. She called her garage too but they too did not answer. Three men who were driving past saw Rashmi and stopped their car beside hers. Two of them got off from their car and helped Rashmi push her car to a corner. They then asked her if she wanted a lift. Rashmi found them decent looking and got into their car.

Once the car was on a lonely street, they stopped the car and raped her. They then threw her on the street after removing credit cards and cash from her handbag. A middle-aged man spotted a bleeding Rashmi and immediately rushed her to the hospital.

The police found out Rashmi's details and informed Raj. Raj was shocked to see Rashmi's face that had been slit and her lips torn. The doctors operated on Rashmi with the consent of Raj. Raj then informed Rashmi's parents and left the hospital.

Rashmi saw herself floating while her body was being operated on and beside her was Sai. Sai whom she had never believed in was smiling at her. Rashmi asked him what was happening and if she would survive. She spoke of her dreams to Sai.

Sai smiled and questioned her that was that all she wanted out of her life, success and fame?

Rashmi nodded. Sai then showed Rashmi how Raj had left her and was picking up his belongings from her house. Next instant Rashmi could see her parents in their car. Her mother was sobbing and crying out to Sai. Her father was chanting, Sai's name and her brother was reading the Sai Satcharitra. They were all pleading to Sai for Rashmi's life.

'What do you see?' asked Sai

'My parents are pleading for my life, they are calling out to you,' said Rashmi and began weeping.

When she looked around there was no Sai, 'I am sorry Sai, I am sorry Sai...' Rashmi cried and when she woke up she saw her family beside her.

Rashmi told her family how Sai had shown her the right path and apologised to her parents. A few days after being released from the hospital, Rashmi requested her parents to take her to Shirdi before going to Nashik.

Quitting her job and starting a life in Nashik, Rashmi became an ardent bhakta of Sai and within few months found herself talking to Sai. Rashmi dedicated her life to the service of the needy.

MORAL: Don't get so engrossed in your work that you forget your duty towards your parents.

True love

Ghafar loved Shila, a Hindu girl whom he had met at the fair in their village. Their friendship grew with time and they messaged each other often. Ghafar wished to marry Shila but Shila did not want to give grief to her parents by marrying a boy who was not of the same religion.

Ghafar spoke to his mother and father about Shila. In a fit of rage Dawood slapped his son and said that there was no way a Hindu girl would step into their home. After a week Ghafar found out about Shila's engagement. A broken hearted Ghafar, left the village.

Ghafar wandered for days till he reached the Ghats of Kashi. He sat there silently watching the dead bodies being cremated. He wept for his love and had not eaten for days.

An old man dressed in white lungi and kurta came and sat beside him.

'You are sad because your girlfriend got engaged?' asked the old man.

Ghafar was stunned by the old man's words.

'How do you know?' asked Ghafar.

'I know everything for everything is in Me,' responded the old man. 'Soon you will find someone who is meant to be with you, go back home Ghafar,' the old man commanded.

Ghafar bowed at the man's feet and went back home and joined his father in his cycle repair shop.

One day a young beautiful girl, Shabnam came to repair her cycle in his cycle repairing shop. It was at that instant the old man's words came back to his mind. And what he said came out true. After their wedding Shabnam and Ghafar visited Shirdi.

As Ghafar was about to enter a restaurant to eat lunch, he saw the old man, he had met in Kashi. Ghafar walked towards the old man.

'You found your love finally, didn't you?' the lungi clad man asked Ghafar.

'You are here in Shirdi?' Ghafar exclaimed falling at his feet.

'I am everywhere,' laughed the old man.

Ghafar asked him to wait as he wanted to introduce him to Shabnam.

When Ghafar returned with Shabnam and told her about the old man Shabnam cried with joy, 'Sai's leelas are amazing, it is thanks to him that we met each other, you are so lucky Ghafar that Sai gave you darshan.'

Shabnam wept with joy as she placed her head on the floor where the old man had stood. Shabnam knew that the old man was none other than her Sai.

MORAL: Sometimes a person may seem like the right partner, but destiny has other plans for you.

Don't be disheartened when the love of your life moves away. Believe that there is someone out there for you. Don't lose hope and keep your faith.

Sai visits Jagdish's home

Dhvani was seething in pain as she lay on the floor of her hut. Her husband Jagdish a devout follower of Sai Baba prayed day and night to Sai for a miracle. Jagdish was unable to see his wife suffer. He felt guilty as he did not have enough funds to treat his wife's cancer and there was no way he could take her to a hospital as it was raining very heavily. Jagdish cried out to Sai for help.

After a while there was a loud knock at the door and when Jagdish opened the door he saw a young man. Jagdish noticed that the bearded handsome man was dry despite the heavy rain.

'You mind if I take shelter for a while?' asked the young man. Jagdish thought for a while, looked at the man's divine face and sparkling eyes and let the man in.

Jagdish offered him water and asked him to sit. When the young man saw the woman crying in pain, he inquired about her. 'My wife is in severe pain. She is suffering from a terrible disease and we don't have enough money to cure her.' said Jagdish.

'Can I see her?' asked the young man.

Jagdish folded his hands and asked the man if he was a doctor.

'Sort of,' the man replied.

Jagdish was grateful to Sai and bowed in front of the small idol of Sai.

'He has heard your prayers,' the man said looking at the idol. He then sat on the floor beside Dhvani and shut his eyes in meditation. After a few minutes, Dhvani became silent.

Jagdish was nervous and checked his wife's breath to see if she was alive. The young man opened his eyes and looked at Jagdish, 'She will wake up in a while don't worry. Her suffering has been eliminated,' said the man and stood up to leave.

Jagdish could not understand that how was it possible that his wife who had been complaining of pain since the past few days was sleeping so peacefully.

Jagdish fell at the man's feet and thanked him. He asked the man to eat something.

'You feed me every day. I never go hungry,' said the young man and left the hut.

After two hours Dhvani woke up and asked for Sai.

Jagdish was confused. 'Sai?'

'Sai had come. It is he who has cured me,' said Dhvani. 'Sai has asked me to visit Maa Kali's temple.'

MORAL: Sai is ever merciful and kind. Sai can come to you in any form and cure you of your illness. Keep your faith in Sai and your difficulties will disappear.

Whose cooking is better?

Parvati chanted Sai's name as she prepared meals for her husband. Rajendra relished his newly wed wife's cooking and praised her to the skies.

Her mother-in-law Kamala who had never raised her hands in prayer was envious of Parvati. Kamala was not too happy to hear her son praising his wife. The praises were so unbearable that Kamala decided to teach Parvati a lesson. Knowing well that her son suffered from ulcers, Kamala added red chilli powder to the vegetable that Parvati had cooked.

At lunch time, when Rajendra was about to open his tiffin and eat, his colleague Tarun asked Rajendra to exchange his tiffin with him. Tarun did not want to eat the bland diet food his wife had packed for him. Rajendra ate Tarun's food for lunch.

When Rajendra returned home, Parvati apologised to her husband for the spicy vegetable but was relieved to know that he had exchanged his tiffin with Tarun. Parvati thanked Sai, she knew it was her Sai who had intervened and protected her husband.

Kamala on hearing about the exchange of tiffins was upset. Next day Kamala added the chilli powder once again but this time she waited for Parvati to pack the tiffin. When Parvati had packed the tiffin and stepped out of the kitchen, Kamala entered and added red chilli powder into it. In a rush she left the chilli powder on the counter.

When Parvati entered the kitchen to pick the tiffin, she saw the red chilli powder on the counter. She opened the tiffin and took a bite from the vegetable she had packed.

At lunch Parvati served the spicy food to Kamala. As soon as Kamala took a bite she screamed, Parvati handed her some sweets and showed her the bottle of red chilli.

'How could you do this to your own son?' asked Parvati.

'I was unable to accept the fact that my son praises you. All these years I have cooked for him and he has never been grateful to me. He does not care for me,' Kamala sobbed.

Parvati embraced her mother-in-law. How could she have not realized the pain of a mother, she thought to herself. A true devotee of Sai is indifferent to praise or criticism and is incapable of hurting anyone.

Parvati asked Kamala to prepare dinner for her son that evening. She told Kamala that it was her Sai's blessings that Rajendra relished her food.

Kamala prepared meals for her son that evening. As she cooked, she chanted the name of Sai. That evening Rajendra relished the dinner and was surprised to know that his mother had cooked for him. Rajendra bowed at his mother's feet and told her how much he missed her cooking but never asked her to cook to avoid troubling her.

Kamala realised how petty she had been and how blessed she was to have such a loving son and daughter-in-law. From that day onwards Kamala spent her time in chanting the name of Sai and seeking forgiveness.

MORAL: When you chant the name of Sai and prepare your meals they are filled with love and become prasad.

Those who truly love Sai are indifferent to praise or criticism.

Dhanwanti and her family

Dhanwanti a mother of two teenage sons, spent most of her time looking after the needs of her husband and children. She was a believer of Sai and worshipped him devoutly. On the other hand, her sons spent most of their time on their mobiles and made fun of Dhanwanti's religious beliefs and practices. Dhanwanti was ridiculed by her husband Jay for running after Guru's and saints.

One day Dhanwanti bumped into her school friend Tina. Tina an elite socialite was surprised to hear of Dhanwanti's lifestyle and began influencing Dhanwanti to live a modern and independent life. In awe of Tina's elite behaviour, Dhanwanti began changing her lifestyle too. Tina taught Dhanwanti to love herself first.

But Dhanwanti was so carried away by the new found social life that she began ignoring her duties and spend her time grooming herself and socializing.

Jay was at first happy to see a transformation in Dhanwanti, but with time he realized that his wife was now neglecting her home. The staff lazed around and nothing at home was in order. When Jay tried speaking to Dhanwanti, she fumed at him. Even the children began feeling neglected but Dhanwanti did not care anymore. For when she cared for them, they had ridiculed her.

Dhanwanti was enjoying her new found friends and her social life till reality hit her hard the day she was invited to a party but Tina wasn't. Enveloped by jealousy, Tina began manipulating her elite friends. Slowly Dhanwanti was outcaste by those same social friends.

Unable to understand their changed behaviour and rejection, Dhanwanti went into depression. Jay and the boys tried cheering her but she would not respond. Jay suggested taking Dhanwanti to a counsellor but she refused to go.

Jay did not give up on his wife and began organizing kirtans at his home. The children too participated in the kirtans. But Dhanwanti would sit for a while and go back to her room and sleep. She had lost interest in life and Sai.

But Sai does not give up on his followers and one night Sai appeared in Dhanwanti's dream and reprimanded her for allowing negativity to grip her. He asked her to come to Shirdi with her family the following day.

Next morning when Dhanwanti woke up, Jay brought in a cup of tea for her and her children walked in with a birthday cake. Dhanwanti had completely forgotten that it was her birthday. Dhanwanti told her family about her dream and was surprised to know that they too had thought the same and had made arrangements.

With Baba's blessings Dhanwanti went back to living her earlier life and enjoyed looking after her family. The only difference was that with Baba's blessings the family appreciated Dhanwanti and were now ardent devotees of Sai.

MORAL: Never lose your faith in Sai. He is always working a way out for you. At times it takes longer for your prayers to be answered, so be patient.

Instil good values in your children. Guide them to the path of devotion.

Sai Baba saves Mahank

The promises that Sai makes, he fulfils but do we keep the vows we make to our Sai?

Here is another story revealing Sai's love for his children.

Gayatri and Kailash were ardent devotees of Sai. So was their son Mahank, till he married Priya. Priya did not believe in any saint and was not ready to accept Mahank and his family's belief system. Prayers and devotion were not part of her lifestyle.

Within a few months Priya had changed Mahank's lifestyle too. Mahank and Priya socialized every evening and Mahank who rarely consumed alcohol earlier was now drinking every day. Gayatri and Kailash conveyed their thoughts to Mahank and Priya, guiding them to limit their social life and drink in limit. Upset with her in-laws interference, Priya convinced her husband to move to another apartment.

Priya was not used to being told off and could not compromise on her freedom and friends. Soon the couple moved out to a rented home and Priya began entertaining often in her new home. Mahank was further addicted to drinking and reached late to office everyday. Kailash was upset with his son for ignoring the business that he had built with hard work and dedication.

Gayatri prayed to her Sai to guide Mahank and Priya towards the right direction. Gayatri worried about Mahank's health too as Sai had warned her that he would suffer.

Gayatri told Mahank about her dream and Sai's instructions. Mahank's intelligence had been clouded and his desire for alcohol was not letting him see his Sai. Sai who had fulfilled his wish of marrying Priya, the love of his life. Mahank had promised Sai that he would always obey his parents command but Mahank had forgotten his promise of respect and love towards his parents.

Mahank argued with his father that in the business world it was all about networking, trying hard to justify his social life. Kailash reminded Mahank that he grew this business without being friends to any elite nor entertaining anyone but with hard work and dedication.

One night, Sai came into Mahank's dream and reminded him of his vow. Next morning when Mahank woke up he could not recollect his dream.

Few weeks later when Mahank went to visit his parents along with Priya, he suddenly felt a severe pain in his chest. His breathing was heavy and his vision was blurring. Mahank cried out to Sai for help and fell unconscious.

Priya dialled for an ambulance while Gayatri rushed to her altar and brought udi and consecrated water. Kailash held onto his son and chanted the name of Sai until the ambulance arrived. Gayatri then rubbed Sai's udi on her son's chest and sprinkled the holy water on him.

Within a few minutes Mahank woke up and sat up as if nothing had happened. He was taken to the hospital but the doctor was unable to detect anything. Mahank knew instantly that it was Sai who had saved him.

Mahank gave up on his drinks and parties, although Priya was unhappy at first with her husband's decision but with time she understood that Sai was protecting and guiding their family.

MORAL: A balance in life is necessary. Do not shy away from devotion and faith. Fall at the feet of Sai and seek his guidance.

Your body is a temple where the soul resides. Don't misuse and abuse that temple.

The man who abused

Tongue is a multi-purpose organ used for taste and speech. Weigh your words carefully before you utter them as you are accountable for every word spoken. Once uttered, they cannot be taken back.

There was once a man named Sunder, who used foul language and abused people. His family members detested his presence. His wife Radhika too tried her best to change him, but failed. Sunder spilled venom, hurting people and making them feel worthless. Radhika prayed religiously to Sai to help her husband change.

One day dressed in tatters, an old man in kafni, stood by Sunder's office gate. When Sunder stepped out of the car to enter the building, he approached Sunder and asked for alms. Sunder in a fit of rage abused the beggar and pushed him away, not knowing that it was Sai.

The old man laughed loudly at Sunder.

'Are you laughing at me? Are you making fun of me you beggar,' Sunder yelled.

Sunder's face flushed red with anger as he heard the old man laughing louder and louder. Sunder told the watchman to beat up the man outside who was laughing loudly. The watchman looked at Sunder surprised, for he could not hear anyone laugh.

That very night Sai came in Sunder's dream in the same form that Sunder had seen him in the day. Sai held Sunder by his neck and began pressing hard till white froth formed outside his mouth. Sunder asked for Sai to forgive him and Sai asked for dakshina. Sunder gave him a five hundred rupee note.

Next morning when Sunder woke up, he felt severe pain in his throat. His mouth was covered with his own spit. He told his wife about his dream. Radhika told him that it was Sai's leela and the ever-merciful Sai was guiding him.

When Sunder arrived at his office, he found the beggar standing by the pole. Sunder stepped out of his car and walked towards the beggar. When he was close to the tattered clothed man, he belched and thanked Sunder for the five hundred rupee note. 'I got myself a good breakfast this morning,' said the man.

Sunder stood stunned unable to comprehend that was this a dream or was what he experienced last night a dream?

'That snake around your neck is hissing again,' said Sai and laughed loudly. Sunder abused the beggar once again and walked into the office building. Unable to focus at work, Sunder walked out of his office looking for the beggar. After hunting for him for a while, he found the old man sitting by the corner. 'So the snake is not letting you be in peace?' asked Sai.

Sunder asked him who he was and why was he doing this to him?

'Pray to Lord Shiva to release you from your curse,' said the man and walked away.

On hearing this Radhika insisted that they visit Lord Shiva's temple every Monday and in a few months there was a change in him.

MORAL: The removal of the venom was the removal of the curse that this man had been subjected to in his earlier birth. Curses can be obstacles in our present life and through Baba's mercy Sunder was freed from his curse.

Mahendra in Kashi

Mahendra a simple devoted man left his family, his wife, son and daughter-in-law as he was troubled by their constant fights. Mahendra went away to Kashi to die a peaceful detached death with the hope of attaining liberation.

Mahendra spent his time meditating in Kashi. His son Rachit pleaded to his father to come back, so did his wife Rukmini but Mahendra listened to no one. When Mahendra had suggested to Rukmini to live with him in Kashi she had agreed at first but then refused. An angry Mahendra stopped talking to his wife for disrespecting his wish. Rukmini tried to explain to her husband that her Sai did not wish for her to go as it was not the right time.

After a few months of living in Kashi, Mahendra received the news of the untimely death of his son. Mahendra who had seen many a dead bodies in Kashi was unable to accept the death of his son.

Mahendra had believed that by living away from his family he had detached himself . But the truth was he hadn't. Rukmini consoled her husband .

It was not in running away from the family but living with the family that one can learn to detach themselves. Rukmini accepted her son's death with the belief that Sai was with him. On the other hand Mahendra could not easily accept the death of his son. Mahendra lived all his life with guilt of not being present when his son breathed his last.

MORAL: Wisdom is attained by living in the world. A householder does not need to run away from his duties to gain wisdom. Detachment should be learnt by living with attachment.

Let your tears flow at the feet of Sai,
In those tears you will find joy,
Sing and dance, for He is with you,
Believe in Sai and His creation,
Take time out to pray to Him,
Take time out to sing to Him,
Take time out to talk to Him,
Ever merciful Sai will fulfil your desires.

Madhav and Rajshri

Madhav along with his wife Rajshri visited Shirdi every month and did parayan (reading) of Sai Satcharitra and stayed there for a week.

Rajshri had been unwell when she arrived into Shirdi but with the application of vibhuti she managed to complete her reading and could stand in queue for darshan everyday.

On the last day as they were loading their luggage in the car to return home, Rajshri requested Madhav that she wanted to meet Baba one last time. Madhav agreed and they stood in the queue for Sai darshan in the Samadhi Mandir.

As they approached Sai's altar, Rajshri could see her Sai smiling. Tears rolled down her eyes as she told her husband that Sai was calling out to her. Madhav did not understand what Rajshri was saying for he could not see what she was describing.

Rajshri told Madhav that Sai is calling out to her and it was time to go. Madhav was perplexed. His wife's face was pale, her eyes brimmed with tears but on her face was a huge grin.

They bowed at the padukas and the moment they stepped outside Rajshri collapsed.

Madhav held his wife in his arms. An ambulance was called and Rajshri was taken to the nearest hospital. Rajshri opened her eyes and told Madhav that Sai had fulfilled her desire.

Madhav knew how his wife had always longed to breathe her last at the feet of Sai and she did.

MORAL: When a Sai bhakta leaves his mortal body, Sai comes to receive him/her.

Real or unreal,
Whatever be the reason,
The world is only an illusion.

You are a traveller on this earth,
Soon you will be back,
In the abode of the Divine,
Answerable for your deeds.

Re-evaluate how you wish to,
Spend the rest of your life,
Wasting it or utilizing every minute,
towards self-realization.

Tanushree reads the Satcharitra

Tanushree and her older brothers lived with their parents. They spent time together and were happy. Life changed when Tanushree's older brother got married and Madhuri came into their home. Madhuri was an egoistic and spoilt girl who hailed from an elite family. Her behaviour at times made Tanushree angry but no one told Madhuri anything, not even her parents.

When Tanushree spoke to her mother, she was told to keep her mouth shut as they did not wish to disturb the peace in their home. On few occasions Madhuri was very rude. Disturbed by their daughter-in-law's comments Tanushree's parents decided to move to an apartment that they had invested in. The apartment was small and far away from the city. When Tanushree heard about it she was upset with her parents for not standing up in front of Madhuri and her brother Tarun.

An upset Tanushree went to her friend Raksha's home and stayed with her that night. The next morning Tanushree saw her friend sitting by the altar and reading a book.

When Raksha had finished her reading Tanushree asked her what she was reading. On finding about the benefits of reading the Satcharitra, Tanushree decided to read it.

She bought herself the book and a small idol of Sai Baba. On the seventh day of her reading Madhuri fainted. She was immediately rushed to the hospital. Tanushree pleaded Sai to be merciful and told him that she did not wish ill for Madhuri.

Those few days of Madhuri's hospitalization the family stood with her like a rock. Their love and kindness towards her had Madhuri realize how mean she had been to her in-laws and Tanushree.

On being discharged she thanked the family and pleaded them not to move to another apartment and asked for forgiveness.

MORAL: Even an evil mind is tamed by Sai's blessings. Reading the Satcharitra helps overcome any obstacle.

Mock not those who have less than you,
For they may lack in wealth but they have values,
Mocking others is not right.

Backbiting others does not help you,
When you bad mouth others,
You are but clearing their debts.

Be happy and let others be happy too,
Beware of what you do,
You never know,
what is in store for you.

Manvi and her mother

From being scolded for her skin colour, to her laugh, to her dress sense Manvi was ridiculed by her mother, Usha. She expected her family to be perfect so that she could flaunt them to her friends. Usha loved talking about her skills in running her home and raising her children. Usha bloated with pride when she was applauded for her skills at cooking, sewing, gardening....

Manvi was not interested in social acceptance nor in wasting time in grooming herself, which led to a clash between her and her mother. Unlike her mother who was popular amongst her friends, Manvi was a loner.

However hard Manvi tried her mother would find faults in her. One day as Manvi was passing by a temple, she heard a group of people singing. Mesmerized by the singing she walked into the temple where she saw the devotees worshipping Sai Baba. Manvi felt so relaxed that she began visiting the temple everyday and staring at the idol of Sai.

When Usha found out about Manvi's daily visit to the temple she discouraged her from idol worship. Manvi stopped going to the temple but prayed to Sai everyday.

One day while Manvi was returning from school, her auto was hit by a car and she was badly injured. Few days had passed and there had been no improvement in Manvi's condition.

Usha thought of the temple that Manvi spoke about and visited it. She stood in front of the life size idol of Sai and wept bitterly. One of the volunteers at the temple comforted Usha and when she told her about her daughter's plight she was guided to their Guru at the temple.

Usha met the Master who was known for his healing powers. Bowing to him she wept and told him about her daughter's plight. 'Within a week's time your daughter will be fine,' said the Master and asked her to seek forgiveness from Sai Baba every day.

After a week of prayers, Usha was told that Manvi had begun responding and had moved her hands. Usha was grateful to Sai and seeing this miracle, went to the temple in the morning and in the evenings.

When Manvi was discharged out of the hospital, Usha took her to the temple to thank the Guru. 'It is Sai's blessing that your Manvi is back from the claws of death,' said the Guru.

The whole family found themselves indebted to Sai Baba for their life. They visited the temple every day and brought in an idol of Sai Baba into their house. Usha, who would never worship any idol or visit any temple, had found new faith.

MORAL: If it were not for Manvi's suffering, Usha would have never changed. Sai has his ways to lead his devotees to the right path.

Peer pressure

As a young girl Pallavi had been a devout follower of Sai Baba. After her marriage to Sailesh her life changed completely. Her husband and in-laws were atheists and slowly Pallavi too gave up on her devotion. Pallavi had to keep up to the standards of her new family and to spend a lot of time in grooming herself and organising social events. Pallavi was blessed with three daughters but she rarely spend time with them. She would be busy entertaining her husband's business associates and family.

Nysha tried many a times talking to her mother Pallavi about the issues she was facing with friends but Pallavi never had the time.

Nysha was in her teens and her younger siblings were ten and seven years old. Unable to share her pain with anyone, Nysha ended up finding solace in chatting with strangers online. One such boy she befriended was Amir who would ask her to do things that were not right. Nysha agreed to meet Amir personally at a café.

Pallavi had no idea who her daughter was meeting, all she knew was that Nysha needed the driver to meet friends and Pallavi provided her daughter with a car and driver. Nysha waited for Amir at the café anxiously. It would be the first time she was meeting a guy alone. Out of nowhere a young woman in her thirties came and sat beside Nysha. Nysha politiely asked the young blonde haired woman to move, as she was expecting a friend. The woman introduced herself as Asha and began chatting and asked Nysha if she was waiting for a boy called Amir. Nysha was stunned and asked Asha who she was. Asha smiled and told her that she was an old friend of her mother Pallavi.

On seeing Amir approaching, Asha stood up and commanded Nysha to not make the mistake of drinking anything that was served and not go anywhere alone with him.

Nysha was confused as to what the woman was trying to tell her and how did she know Amir. While her mind was asking questions, Amir kissed Nysha on her cheek and sat beside her and began chatting. He then ordered snacks and iced tea and then excused himself. As soon as he left Asha walked towards Nysha and asked her to go back home. Nysha was now irritated with this lady and asked her to mind her own business. But Asha did not give up and sat on the table beside Nysha's, staring at her.

The waiter brought in their order, smiled at Amir and left. Nysha and Amir conversed as they snacked on the sandwich. Amir asked Nysha to go for a drive with him after she finished the iced tea. Nysha moved her gaze towards Asha who was signalling her not to go.

Nysha sensed there was something wrong with the drink and excused herself with the pretext of visiting the washroom. From there, Nysha called her driver and then scrambled towards her car.

When Nysha opened her eyes, Pallavi was sitting beside her. 'What's the matter Nysha? What happened to you?' Pallavi asked her daughter.

Nysha told Pallavi all that had happened and what the lady had stated.

Pallavi felt herself being protected by Sai's grace and told Nysha that the person she had met was none other than her Sai.

MORAL: Sai is always by your side, reminding you of his presence. You may get involved in your life and forget him. But he never forgets those who have even placed a leaf at his feet with love.

As you queue outside My shrine,
I watch you with open eyes,
You may not see me from afar,
But my eyes are fixed on each of you,
I can see your pleading eyes,
I can hear your cries,
I can sense your pain,
And before you reach ME,
I have already answered your prayers.

Mahi and her new shoes

Mahi walked barefoot to school everyday. Her only pair of slippers had torn and her parents could not afford another pair. They could barely manage to acquire two meals for the day. At the municipal school Mahi was teased and laughed at by her school mates and at times by the teacher.

One day Mahi sat by the field and wept and prayed to God for a pair of shoes. A young man who was passing by stood by her and asked her if he could help her in anyway. Mahi at first refused to talk to the stranger but then told him about how she was made fun at by her friends in school.

Sai who had come in the form of a dark young man blessed her and told her that your cries have reached Sai, he will give you what you desire.

Mahi smiled and asked him how would Sai know? 'Because Sai is within you and he can hear you,' said the young man.

Mahi was confused by his reply. She bid him bye and walked towards her home. After walking a few steps Mahi stopped to turn around to ask the man how could Sai be within her and if he was, where did he reside? But when Mahi turned he was not to be seen. Mahi thought he might have disappeared in the fields and she walked towards her home with the belief that Sai would fulfil her desire.

When she reached her hut, Mahi told her mother Pankhi about the man who told her that Sai would fulfil her wish.

Pankhi laughed at the innocence of her daughter and said, 'We don't have enough money to fill your stomach, how will we cover your feet?'

Mahi told her mother that she had faith that what the young man told her would come true. Mahi sat outside her hut waiting for Sai.

After a while she saw her father walking towards their hut. On his back was a sack. Mahi ran towards her father. He embraced her and from the large sack removed a pair of shoes and showed to Mahi. Mahi tried the shoes and they fit perfectly.

Pankhi came out of the hut on hearing her daughter screaming in excitement and she asked her husband Damu from where he got the shoes and what did the large sack contain.

He told her the story of how a young man was passing by the fields and was thirsty. Damu gave water to the thirsty man, who in return gave him money. When Damu refused the money, the man walked towards his car. The man walked back with a whole sack of clothes and shoes that he was asked by Sai to give to the one who quenched his thirst.

Mahi thanked Sai and wore her new shoes to school the next day. With the grace of Sai, Mahi grew upto be a doctor and found joy in helping others. Mahi had made a promise to Sai that she would bring joy to the faces of those children who were unprivileged as she had been.

MORAL: If Sai has blessed you with riches, do charity. If you are blessed with knowledge, share it. Distribute food to the hungry. Educate those that are not fortunate enough. Treat all equally.

Lord Ganesha

Murlidhar and his family celebrated the Ganpati festival every year.

In the year 2020 the family was confused about whether to welcome Ganpati in their home or not. Murlidhar's son Jignesh was not keen to celebrate Ganpati that year as he did not wish his parents to be at risk.

But Murlidhar and Swati were keen to celebrate. They could not stop the tradition of bringing Ganesha, worshipping him, and then immersing him in the river. Lord Ganesha came in Murlidhar's dream and asked him if he brought his idol home to please others or pray?

Confused by his dream Murlidhar woke his wife up and told her about his dream. To which she responded that they would worship the Ganesha idol that was on their altar.

Murlidhar argued with his wife that the celebration was all about bringing a new idol home, worshipping, and immersing it.

Festivals were reasons to spend time with family and celebrate life. Theoretically, one should celebrate every day of their life. The man not convinced went to his balcony, shut his eyes, and asked for guidance from Ganesha again.

The dark clouds had moved away and when he opened his eyes he saw an impression of Ganesha on the moon. He bowed his head in reverence and questioned, 'What do I do?' Murlidhar heard his inner voice, 'is there any difference how big your idol is or whether it is immersed in the river or sea? If you truly wish to immerse, surrender your bad qualities at my feet. You can also immerse my idol in water and keep me back on your altar. In that immersion, I will take upon myself your obstacles and vices.'

Hearing his inner voice, Murlidhar made a decision. He would celebrate Ganpati Utsav with his present idol and do so with devotion. It did not matter if their extended family and friends would not be able to join him.

MORAL: Surrender yourself at his feet, Lord Ganesh will take away all your problems.

Rejoice in the beauty of the Universe,
Celebrate your birth,
Small hurdles will come your way,
But look at the larger picture,
Count your blessings not your loss,
Count what you have,
Innumerable lives you have led,
Many lessons you have learnt,
And choice to attain liberation,
Isn't that reason enough to celebrate?

You cry for obstacles that come your way,
The obstacles that will pass away,
Seek not material wealth,
Fear not emotional health,
If you surrender at his feet,
Everything that bothers you will disappear.

Tahira and Sai

There are some who after receiving grace and blessings from Sai, forget him. They are attracted towards the dark faculties. What are these dark faculties? These are those habits and feelings that take you away from the positive, from your Sai, from your Master, from the Truth, from Allah Malik.

Tahira visited and worshipped Lord Shiva for many years. Once a year the family visited Shirdi too. Once Tahira joined college, she found herself seeking attention from boys. Her friends spent most of their time in bars and restaurants. Tahira who never drank or ate non vegetarian food, dropped her religious beliefs to please her friends. She feared that if she didn't fit in, they would ignore her. Tahira began dressing differently and attracted male attention.

Pankaj a close friend of Tahira and to whom she was attracted to, invited her home for his birthday. He pleaded to Tahira to spend the day with him in his apartment. At first Tahira refused the invitation but after his constant messages she agreed to visit him at his home. Tahira had no idea what Pankaj was planning to do.

She lied to her parents about going for the seminar with friends in the train and returning back with all of them, so they had no reason to be concerned.

Pankaj had asked his room-mates to stay out and not enter the apartment until he called them. Once he had drugged her, he would call them. The moment Tahira reached she felt uneasy and regretted her decision. She liked

Pankaj but was not too comfortable with his behaviour. The apartment had a peculiar smell that made Tahira sick.

Tahira excused herself and headed to the washroom. She dialled her father's number but could not get through. She called her mother but she did not answer. She prayed to Shiva for help. Tahira had given out wrong signals to Pankaj in college and regretted accepting to come so far and lying to her parents.

Building up courage Tahira walked out of the washroom. Pankaj lay on the couch. Tahira sat on the couch beside Pankaj. In her mind she continued praying to Lord Shiva for guidance. Pankaj drew closer to Tahira. Tahira requested him to give her some time. Pankaj then asked her to sip from the drink to calm her nerves.

Just when Tahira was about to sip on the drink, the doorbell rang. Pankaj jumped off the couch and headed to the door and peeped through the eye hole. He saw a middle-aged man. Pankaj opened the door to ask him who he was and why he was ringing his bell.

'I have come to take my daughter,' said the wavy-haired man and pushed himself in.

Tahira rushed to her father and gave him a tight hug and cried. How did her father know that she was here? She had left no address with them.

'How did you find me?' asked Tahira in the car.

'You called me,' said Amar.

Tahira thought for a moment, she had called her father but it had not gone through.

Tahira stared at her father whose face was glistening. He had not asked her any questions nor reprimanded her for lying.

Amar dropped Tahira at the lobby and said, 'I have to go to work.'

'I am sorry dad, I lied to you.'

'Don't ever lie and don't ever see that boy again,' said Amar and took the car away.

Tahira walked up the steps to her house and rang the house bell.

'Tahira you are back so early?' asked Amar opening the door of the house.

Tahira was taken aback and stood still for a few minutes.

'Didn't you just drop me?' she asked her father.

'Drop?' asked Amar.

Confused with what had just happened Tahira went to her room and shut the door. She stood by her window sill and looked at her parking spot. Their car was standing below. Tahira shut her eyes and thanked her Lord Shiva for help.

MORAL: Never lie to your family. Never get carried away by your friends. Believe in yourself and in who you are. Don't let anyone tell you otherwise. It does not matter if your friends don't accept you. Choose your friends wisely.

Tahira was saved by Sai who came in the form of her father.

Saved by Sai

After losing his wife to cancer, Deepak was lonely and stayed alone in his apartment in Mumbai. His son Amit insisted that his father keep a full-time servant and appointed one before leaving for Canada.

Deepak was guilty of treating his wife poorly while she was alive and decided to spend his time praying for forgiveness. Deepak visited the Sai temple beside his home daily and spent his mornings gazing at the idol of Sai and singing to him.

One morning Deepak heard the voice of Sai asking him to go home. Not too sure if that was really Baba or someone at the temple, Deepak looked around. Few devotees were engrossed in their prayers. No one was talking. Once again, he heard a voice, 'Deepak go home.' Deepak stood up and walked down the steps. As he was about to get off the last step, he slipped and sprained his ankle.

Ashok who was walking into the temple saw Deepak and rushed towards him. Ashok insisted that he drop Deepak to his building which was close by.

Deepak rang the bell to his apartment, but the servant did not open the door. Deepak handed his house key to Ashok and he opened the door. As soon as the house door flung open, they saw that the servant Shambu was holding a knife in one hand and a duffel bag in the other.

Ashok flung himself on Shambu and pulled the knife from his hand. Tying him with a rope, Ashok called the police and Shambu was taken away. Deepak was shocked to see that his servant had opened his locker and was about to run away with his wife's jewellery and cash.

Ashok called his wife Meena who was a doctor and she attended to Deepak's sprain and cooked for him. The couple looked after Deepak for a few days till he found himself an honest servant.

Deepak visited the temple after a week and when he sat in front of Sai, Sai told him that it was his constant prayers that had saved him from being robbed.

MORAL: Our constant prayers can save us from our bad karmas. At times we are meant to bear the brunt of our karmas but when Sai intervenes the degree of the punishment gradually decreases.

Don't be attached to material gains. What is meant for you will be yours, what is not will never be fruitful even if you gain it through manipulation. That kind of wealth will slip from your hands like sand from your palms.

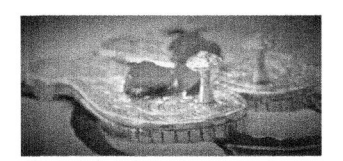

Dandekar and his family

Kishore Dandekar was a successful business man and often travelled abroad for his business. While he was away from his family he would indulge in wrong actions. Manvi his wife was a devotee of Sai. She had doubts on her husband's fidelity and prayed to Sai to safeguard her family.

Kishore had intimate relations with another woman in a foreign country. He provided this woman with a home and payed for her expenses. On one trip Kishore did not inform his mistress of his arrival as he wanted to surprise her. When he reached there, he found her with his business associate. In a fit of rage, Kishore threw his girlfriend out of his house.

Guilty of cheating on his wife for his disloyal girlfriend, Kishore decided to commit suicide. Just when he was about to head to the balcony, he received a call from his wife Manvi. Manvi told Kishore how much she and the children were missing him and awaiting his return home. When Kishore put the phone down, he realized that he was about to commit a grave mistake and decided to confess the truth to his wife when he went back to India.

On reaching India he told Manvi the truth. On hearing about her husband's mistress Manvi was upset and asked her husband for a divorce. Manvi then began ignoring her husband and slept in another room.

One night, Baba came in Manvi's dream and questioned her about her decision. Manvi told Baba that she could not be with a man who had cheated on her. On waking up Manvi tried to remember Baba's response but could not recollect what he had said.

Manvi asked Kishore to find her another apartment and the day Manvi was packing to leave, Kishore had a massive heart attack. Manvi could not stop herself from tending to her husband. During those days of his suffering, Manvi realized how much she loved Kishore.

Kishore pleaded for forgiveness everyday from Manvi. But Manvi had made up her mind that even if she loved him, she had to leave. Kishore had cheated on her once and he would do it again.

The next morning when Manvi sat in her prayer room and was praying to Baba she heard his voice, 'you call yourself my bhakta, but you don't listen to me. If you don't forgive your husband, you will never be forgiven for births to come. Not forgiving is a bigger sin, for you will carry this baggage for ever.'

Manvi looked up at her Sai's idol and cried to him that it was not so easy to forgive someone who had breached your trust.

But Sai's word was law for Manvi and she agreed to accept and forgive her husband. Few years down the line Manvi's life changed. Kishore loved her and tended to her every need. Her children got the best of education and their business flourished.

MORAL: Forgiving others faults will break the karmic cycle of births. Don't judge others for their mistakes. Only a forgiving person can be close to Sai. Those who live with grudge, anger and hatred live a life of sin.

Soumya's suffering

Life is a journey that we undertake to evolve as souls. Our soul has taken many births to learn lessons.

Anil worked in a government job. The commute from his home to work was long and he would come back home tired, the frustration of which he removed on his wife Soumya.

Their two children were in their teens and one was giving his tenth boards and the other was in the eleventh. Their expenses were high and Anil being an honest man, never did any wrong dealings. Soumya wanted a better life for herself and tried to speak to Anil to find a better job but he would not listen to her.

It was one morning that Soumya's good friend asked her to join her for a prayer meeting, a satsang. Soumya had no time and too much work at home but her friend Janu insisted, as the home where the satsang was being held was close by. Soumya agreed and walked along with Janu into the building. Soumya could hear voices of ladies singing.

Soumya looked at the idol that the ladies were praying to in the living room. Sai was smiling at her. Throughout the kirtan Soumya could not move her eyes away from Sai's smiling face and love filled eyes.

After the kirtan was over, Soumya stood in the line with the other ladies to bow to the idol and collect prasad. When Soumya bowed in front of Sai, a flower that had been sitting near Sai's lap fell on her lap. Soumya picked up the flower and walked towards her friend Janu. Janu was chatting with the hostess, Puja. Soumya showed them the flower and Puja told her that she should keep it as it was a blessing from Sai. Janu told Soumya that good things would soon come her way.

Soumya hoped what the women said came true. With prasad in her hands Soumya rushed home while Janu stayed back to chit chat about Sai and his miracles with her friends.

When Soumya reached home, she kept the flower in a book. Soumya had no altar in her house. She never prayed and rarely visited temples.

That night when her husband came home, he was frustrated and expressed his desire to quit his job. Soumya was worried for her husband and was unable to sleep at night. They had very little savings and if Anil gave up on his job how would they manage.

Next morning forcing herself to wake up Soumya went about her household work. It was a Sunday and Anil suggested they go to a park. But Soumya was too upset and worried about Anil's job.

'If you give up on your job Anil and don't find another one, how are we going to survive?' Soumya asked her husband. Anil assured Soumya that he would not quit till he found another job. Soumya was not convinced and feared Anil's impulsive nature.

After lunch when everyone was resting Soumya picked her phone and looked for Sai bhajans on You tube. Many bhajans were listed and Soumya listened to them and thought of the merciful eyes of Sai, that she had seen at Puja's home.

She heard a line, 'He will keep you in his shade, why you worry. When his mercy is on you, why you worry.' Soumya wept. She thought of how her life had been comfortable before marriage but from the time she married Anil, life had been a struggle. They rarely went out to eat. The boys had their demands of money and Soumya found it difficult to save. With tears rolling down her cheeks Soumya folded her hands and asked Sai to bless her family.

Next day when Anil was on his way to work in the train, a middle-aged man in a suit sat beside him and introduced himself as Gope. Anil shared his frustration with Gope, who listened attentively. After listening to Anil for a while, Gope handed a business card to Anil and asked him to call this company and speak to Hemant. The train halted and Gope alighted from the train.

Anil reached his office and dialled the number on the card. The lady at the reception held the line a few seconds and then responded, 'email us your CV and you can come and meet Hemant Sir, this afternoon.'

Anil immediately sent his CV and left early to meet Hemant. Hemant greeted Anil and told him that their employee had quit today and he was looking for someone with qualifications, like Anil. Anil was offered the job with a double pay of what he was earning.

Hemant asked him how he got his number. When Anil told Hemant how it happened, Hemant smiled for he knew it was a miracle of Sai. Hemant was a devout follower of Sai. When Anil reached home and told Soumya. Soumya broke down into tears and told Anil that it surely was Sai in the train whom he had met. Anil was surprised for Hemant too had spoken about Sai. Both Anil and Soumya decided to go to Shirdi. Soumya built a small altar in her home with an idol of Sai and their life changed for the better.

MORAL: You may have not yet met Sai, but Sai knows you since births. He is always protecting you. Call out to him, he will be there for you.

Zohaib comes to Mumbai

Zohaib earned a meagre amount in his small town and supported his parents, brothers and sister. His father a farmer had been crippled when hit by a truck while crossing the highway and Zohaib began farming on the land. His younger brothers helped him. But Zohaib was not too happy farming and prayed to Allah to help him out. He was unable to toil in the heat and wondered how his father worked for so many years.

After a few months a business man offered Zohaib a good amount for his land. After consulting his father Zohaib sold off the land. With a good amount in the bank as security for his family, Zohaib decided to move to Mumbai to make a living. After reaching Mumbai, Zohaib learnt driving and found himself a job as a chauffeur.

The fast life of Mumbai changed Zohaib. His calls to his parents became infrequent and after work Zohaib headed to a bar surrounded by women. One day on his way back home a drunk Zohaib rammed his bicycle into a bus and was beaten by the bus driver. The police too thrashed him and Zohaib was taken to the police station and released the following day.

Zohaib went back to work to be told that he had been fired. A servant handed over the envelope of his due salary. When Zohaib asked the servant the reason of his dismissal he told him that the bosses did not want a drunken man as a driver.

Zohaib walked aimlessly for a few days praying to Allah to forgive him. One day Zohaib went to a garden and sat on a bench beside an old man.

'Drinking will take you to hell,' said the old man to Zohaib. 'What happened to your promise to Allah?'

Zohaib looked at the bearded old man wearing tattered clothes.

'Who are you?' Zohaib asked, 'and what promise?'

The old bearded man asked Zohaib, 'you got from Allah what you wanted. What have you done in return?'

Zohaib walked home, cleansed himself and rolled his mat and prayed to Allah for forgiveness. In a few days Zohaib had found another job. When he sat in the car of his new employer, a picture of the old man he had met a few days back was hanging on the rear-view mirror. Zohaib's eyes welled up and he asked the owner, 'Who is this man?'

His boss told him he was Sai Baba of Shirdi, a messenger of God.

MORAL: Strange are His ways and blessed are those who are graced by his presence. At times He appears to those who haven't even heard of Him. The ever-merciful Sai Baba loves all equally.

Singing is a pure act that connects you to Sai,
Sing to Sai, for He loves music.

In a sweet tender voice call out to Sai,
Sing His glory, sing Him songs of love.

Sai cannot resist the devotion of his devotees.

Satram

Many are in search of enlightenment, but only those who have patience and faith will understand and find the Truth.

Satram was a devotee who did his naam japa and served the poor. It was Satram's desire to attain liberation and free his soul from the cycles of birth and death.

Satram prayed to his Master to guide him. The Master put up Satram's request to Sai, for his Master could not intervene in the play of the Universe. Sai came to Satram in his dream and asked him to come by the river the following day.

Satram went by the river and on reaching there he was asked to get into a boat. Satram followed the instructions of Sai and hopped onto the wooden boat. When he started rowing the boat, he saw that there were holes in it. Satram feared that he would die and his mind began doubting Sai and his intentions. Satram rowed the boat back to the bank. And when questioned by Sai why he did that Satram had no answer.

It was then that Sai came in his form. Satram fell at Sai's feet. 'This is the reason you will not be able to attain liberation. In your heart there is still doubt. Your mind is still attached to your past traits of doubt. Till you don't let them go, you will never attain liberation,' Sai told Satram.

MORAL: Till we don't surrender completely to Sai we will not be able to attain liberation. Satram believed

that he had cleared of his karmic account but his past samskara of doubt had not been erased.

When obstacles come in our life, our faith wavers. We begin doubting the existence of Sai. We need to overcome the feeling of doubt and keep faith in Sai, only then can we attain liberation.

Kunti and Sai

Kunti was saddened after her husband's death. It had been only a few years into their marriage when Mohandas had died. Kunti thought of giving away her wealth and moving to an ashram.

She prayed to Sai Baba for guidance. Kunti felt lost and did not know what to do with her life.

One night as Kunti wept bitterly, Sai came into her room in the form of her maid and placed his hand on her forehead and with the other he wiped off her tears. He spoke to her, asking her to calm down and that soon she would meet someone who would love her. Kunti was shocked to hear her maid speak this way. 'Daksha, what is wrong with you? please go from here, I don't want to hear anything like this,' she said.

Daksha smiled and left the room. In the morning when Kunti woke up she apologized to Daksha for being rude. 'Last night you came to my room and I was rude to you,' said Kunti. Daksha told her that she never came to her room and that she must have dreamt of her.

'Did you not tell me,' before Kunti could complete her sentence, the door-bell rang.

Daksha opened the door to a young man who asked for Mrs. Mohandas. Kunti walked to the door and asked the man the purpose of his visit, he told her and that he owed her late husband money and had come to hand over the cheque. Kunti let Shailendra in and offered him tea. As they sat to have tea, Kunti heard a voice tell her that

85

Shailendra will look after you. Kunti was confused and upset with herself for thinking such thoughts.

After an hour into conversation with Shailendra, Kunti began feeling lighter and happier. After Shailendra left Kunti sat in her temple and asked Baba if it was Him who was putting these thoughts in her head. In that instance the fragrance of sandalwood filled the temple, a signal from her Baba.

After a year Kunti married Shailendra and lived happily.

MORAL: Baba can come in any form to his devotees.

Rain and storm

Rajesh was on his way home after work on a heavy monsoon day. Due to constant rains the roads were filled with water and his car broke down on the road. Rajesh got off the car and began walking towards his home but the water was too deep and it was dark.

Rajesh called out to his Sai for help. After walking for fifteen minutes in the dirty water he gave up and stood by the side of the road. Just then Dinkar approached him and asked him to come and take rest in his home.

Rajesh called his family from Dinkar's land line and informed them that he was safe. The family was surprised as to how Rajesh had got through, as their house phone had not been working.

Dinkar gave Rajesh a change of clothes and his wife cooked dinner. Next morning, when the rains had subsided Rajesh thanked Dinkar and his wife and went home.

After a week, Rajesh decided to visit the family who had helped him and thank them with a small token. He bought gifts for them and went to the complex. He walked up three floors and headed to the flat where Dinkar lived. It was dark that night but Rajesh clearly remembered walking up a flight of three stairs and then to the far left. The door that had a Ganesh picture outside. When Rajesh walked up to the door, he didn't see the Ganesh picture. He rang the bell and an old man opened the door. Rajesh asked him if this was Dinkar's home and the man said that he had never heard of this name.

Rajesh checked with the security guard also stated that he never heard of anyone called Dinkar.

MORAL: Sai looks after his devotees and they see many miracles. Miracles that may sound untrue to those who don't believe in Sai, but Sai's followers know their Sai's leelas.

Faith can move mountains

Dipti's parents arranged her marriage to Narender. After few weeks into their marriage Narender realized that Dipti was not the kind of girl he had dreamt of. Dipti was too naive and engrossed in house work, while Narender enjoyed a social life and drinking every night.

Dipti longed to spend time with her husband alone but he preferred to go out with friends. A few months into their marriage Narender ignored Dipti and began socializing alone and he began chatting with his old girlfriend Preena.

Narender began abusing Dipti and finding reasons to fight. Dipti tried hard to save her marriage but Narender did not cooperate. Narender's parents kept themselves distant and did not wish to comment on their son's behaviour.

Dipti began fasting on Monday's and prayed to Lord Shiva. One day while she was at the temple, she heard people talk about Shirdi and how one's wishes were fulfilled there. Dipti heard her inner voice nudging her to visit Shirdi.

Dipti requested her in-laws to let her go to Shirdi and they told her that they had no objection if Narender did not mind. Narender was pleased to have his wife out of his way and immediately gave her permission.

Within ten minutes of planning her trip, Dipti received a call from her school friend Meena who told Dipti that she regularly visited Shirdi. Meena made arrangements for Dipti's stay in Shirdi.

Dipti left early next morning in a hired car and after reaching Shirdi she went to the Samadhi Mandir for darshan. That night Dipti dreamt of Lord Shiva and Sai Baba. She saw them merge into one.

When she woke up the next morning, she felt fearless and the week that she stayed in Shirdi she dedicated in service and reading. In that week she had experienced Sai's presence many a times and felt blissful. Dipti went back home with the belief that whatever was meant to be, would happen and that she would go with the flow.

The evening that Dipti reached home, her husband Narender did not return home that night. Her in-laws had suddenly left for Europe to be with their daughter. Dipti was informed by her helper that Narender stayed out every night. Dipti cried in front of her Shiva and Sai and asked them to guide her, for she was not sure if she should work on her marriage or give up.

Next morning when she called her husband, he messaged her back saying that he was busy. Narender did not come home that evening and his phone was switched off. After making calls to his office she found out that Narender had not come to the office.

Later in the day she received a call from the police and was informed that her husband was accused of beating up a man. Dipti called the lawyer and within few days Narender was out on bail.

Ashamed of his behaviour Narender told his wife the truth about his relation with Preena and how he had ended up in a brawl with Preena's husband. Narender felt guilty of reviving his old friendship and asked Dipti for forgiveness. Dipti forgave Narender and together they decided to work on their marriage.

MORAL: Baba has his reasons for asking us to do things. Sometimes our prayers are answered immediately but at times we have to undergo penance before Sai answers our prayers.

Dipti had a score of karmas to clear before she was blessed. Baba let her cleanse her karmas with her prayers and faith. It was her love and devotion to Baba that with time she became a healer and worked for the good of people.

Gayatri's deformity

Gayatri was born with a deformed leg due to which she limped when she walked. Her parents shunned her for two reasons. One for being a daughter and the other for her deformity. Gayatri's older sisters loved Gayatri but her parents Kishan and Babli ridiculed all their daughters. They had four daughters and were ashamed of them. Daughters meant dowry and that worried Kishan and Babli.

While her daughters ran the house, Babli sat in the veranda complaining about her life and her bad luck. Kishan ran a pan beedi shop and did not have enough money to take Gayatri to a good doctor.

The parents sold their sixteen year old daughter to a bald head widowed man with two children. They were paid a good amount for it. The second daughter was forcefully converted to another religion and married off to a man in Saudi Arabia who already had two wives. Their third daughter ran away with a married man whom she loved only to be beaten up by him too.

Gayatri took over the responsibilities of the house once all the sisters had left. She would find odd jobs and help in the running of the house. The small village was near Shirdi and Gayatri heard her fellow companions talk about the temple and how everyone's wishes were fulfilled. One of them handed her a picture of Sai Baba.

Gayatri prayed and worshipped to Sai. After a few years their second daughter Shanti who had been converted to Sakeena after her marriage, visited her parents. Sakeena had not been in touch with her parents but missed Gayatri and had consulted a doctor in Mumbai to correct her sister's deformity.

Babli and Kishin would not let Gayatri go with Sakeena, but when she offered them money they let her take Gayatri. Gayatri requested Sakeena to take her to Shirdi before leaving for Mumbai. Sakeena agreed and they visited Shirdi.

After they completed their darshan and stepped out Gayatri was stopped by a middle-aged man who asked her if her limp was from birth. When Gayatri responded in the affirmative, he suggested her to visit his free clinic in Shirdi for examination.

Sakeena and Gayatri went to the clinic and the doctor after diagnosing told Gayatri that she would be cured, but he had a condition. The condition was that Gayatri would stay in Shirdi for a week and do seva and read the Satcharitra every day. After ten days he would operate her in the nursing home and not charge a penny. One week the sisters visited the temple, read the holy book, attended aartis and joined in the seva. After a week the doctor performed a surgery and within few weeks Gayatri was fine.

MORAL: All diseases can be cured with Sai's blessings. If one desires to serve Sai, He himself paves the path for you.

Smriti and her friends

Since a young age, Smriti spent her life enjoying and rarely took time out for her family. Her good karmas from her past lives had blessed her with prosperity and luxury. But in the present birth, she did not work on her good deeds. Instead she spent her time in idle gossip.

As Smriti grew older, lots of health issues cropped up and her social life came to a standstill. She lost touch with most of her friends and slipped into depression.

Smriti's health worsened as her mind was filled with negative thoughts.

Her grand-children would come to see her but Smriti would be obsessed with grief and tell her children about how her friends had ditched her and that no one gave her time. Her older son and daughter-in-law avoided spending time with her despite being in the same house. The grand-children too began avoiding their grandmother. Smriti would spend her time by herself in her bedroom.

When Smriti's youngest son Suraj and daughter-in-law Mili who lived abroad came to see their mother they were shocked to see Smriti so low and filled with negative thoughts. They took her to a counsellor for treatment.

Smriti refused to talk to any counsellor and was upset that they thought she was mad. Mili a believer of Sai guided her mother-in-law into praying and read the Satcharitra to her every day. When it was time for her to go back she asked Smriti to read the Satcharitra every day.

After Mili and Suraj left, Smirti felt lonely and spent her time reading and praying as Mili had advised her. After a month of reading the Satcharitra, Smriti began seeing a difference in her thoughts. The family found Smriti calmer and happier. Her older son and daughter-in-law and grandchildren began enjoying her company. Her friends too started contacting her. But this time Smriti had made a choice.

MORAL: Prayers are your only saving grace. A simple reading of the Satcharitra changed Smriti's thinking and brought her out of her mental and physical illness.

Aarti's spritual pride

Aarti was from India and after her marriage lived with her husband Chander in Europe. Chander was not into any religious beliefs and detested if his wife spoke of Sai.

Aarti's spiritual life took a back seat for a while as she raised her children. However hard she tried her children would not participate in her daily rituals.

Aarti came to India but her family did not accompany her. While visiting Shirdi, Sai gave darshan to Aarti in the form of a woman and handed her nine coins. She told her that these coins would change her life, condition being she would not bloat in pride. Aarti thanked the woman and left Shirdi.

Aarti returned to her family in Europe and kept the coins in her temple and prayed to them day and night. After a few months Aarti was blessed with a miracle. Her Sai's idol began oozing nectar and Aarti was overjoyed. Her prayers had been answered, her home was blessed.

But Chander and her children laughed at Aarti and did not consider the oozing of honey a miracle. Aarti's friends visited her home to see the miracle. The attention from her friends made her feel special and Aarti began bloating with pride. After a few days the miracle had stopped and Chander laughed at Aarti and her Sai. She argued with Chander and abused him for not understanding the miracles of Sai. Aarti was upset with her husband and walked out of her home and stayed with a friend that night.

Aarti dreamt of Sai that night, 'you were meant to bring a change in your husband's life. By cursing your husband and walking out of your home, you have created a strong tie with him. I had told you clearly not to bloat in pride. You were proud of your devotion and you need to go back to your husband and apologize. Pride is but a downfall of your spiritual growth.'

Aarti woke up ashamed and went back home and apologised. Aarti never forced her beliefs anymore on her family and with time they all became followers of Sai.

MORAL: Each human being chooses their journey. Don't be proud of your spirituality. If someone else does not follow your path don't demean them.

Madhu visits the temple

Madhu walked to school daily and would pass the Lakshmi Narayan temple. Every morning she would stop by to collect prasad from the temple that would sustain her through the day.

Madhu's father spent the entire day sleeping and drinking while her mother Sharda cleaned people's home and then would come home and prepare the food from the essential items received by the temple.

Because of the pandemic the temples were shut. It was not possible for the temple authorities to allow long queues outside the temple. Sharda too had lost her job and they didn't have any money at home. A month had passed and the strict regulations made it difficult for them to survive.

After going hungry for a few days, Madhu walked towards the temple. On her way to the temple Madhu was stopped by a policeman, 'where are you going?' he asked. Madhu told him that they had no food at home and she was going to pray at the temple.

The policeman felt sorry for Madhu and handed her a five hundred rupee note and asked her to go back home as it was not safe. Madhu refused the five hundred rupee note and walked back home dejected.

When she told her mother about the incident, her mother was upset that she had refused money. But Madhu told her mother that she felt that the police constable needed the money more than she did and she was sure that their prayers would be answered.

The next day Madhu set out once again. On her way she recognised one of the volunteers of the temple and went up to him. Standing at a distance she asked him if she could get some food for her and those around her.

The volunteer looked at Madhu and told her that they need not worry as they would be supplying packets of food to their home every day. The volunteer went to his car and handed Madhu packets of grains and snacks.

A contented Madhu slept well that night. In her dream she saw Sai who told her that he was pleased with her for thinking of others and he promised her that she would never go hungry after this day

Madhu woke up next morning cheerful and told her mother about the dream. Sharda realized that although they had been visiting the temple daily to receive grains, they were in reality being blessed by Sai.

MORAL: Even if you enter the temple for your selfish gains, every time you step in you receive blessings. By bowing at His feet, you receive His love and blessings.

Humans bloat with pride,
And argue with might,
They believe they are strong and intelligent,
Ready to fight with conviction.

Alas, when death strikes,
They realize that they are nothing,
without His benediction.

Conversations with Sai

1. **What is a prayer?**

   Prayer is a mode of communication with God, a direct line. You can pray to anyone who you wish to call upon. Sitting in silence is also a form of prayer. Visualizing your deity, guru and invoking them is a prayer. Talking, listening and experiencing the presence of the Supreme is prayer.

2. **What should one communicate?**

   After bowing to your Deity or Sai smile and feel their Light, their energy. Talk to Sai about your feelings and share your worries. Think of Him as your Father, Mother and friend and share your joys and pains.

3. **Will I get what I wish, Sai?**

   That depends on your faith. Will Sai always give what you wish? Yes and No. There will be times when your wishes may not be fulfilled. That does not mean Sai has not heard your prayers, or is incapable of fulfilling your wish.

   At times what you wish for may not be beneficial for you. Surrender to Sai in those moments. Let Sai decide what is good for you. Put out a prayer and surrender to Sai. Believe that you will receive what you desire if it is good for you and that too at the right time.

   'Put in your application and leave it to Sai. Let him decide if it is right for you or no.'

4. **How does Sai listen to all his bhaktas?**

    Sai is omnipresent, omniscient. He is not bound by time or space. He is in every atom and every cell. The one who is everywhere does not need to be only in one place.

5. **Why do I have to go to a temple or Shirdi to see him?**

    When you visit a shrine it adds to your good karmas for you are taking time out from your busy life.

    Secondly, these shrines are filled with positive energy. This effulgent light permeates into your body and fills you with positivity.

6. **What if I don't wish to believe in Sai?**

    Whether you believe or not, it does not change or negate His presence. Sai is within you, for He is Supreme Consciousness. By negating Sai, Sai will not cease to exist.

7. **How should I then spend my day? Should I pray the whole day to please Sai?**

    Spend your day the way you wish to, do your duties, your household chores and socialize with friends. As you go about with your daily living, internally be aware of Sai's presence. Experience him in whatever you do.

8. **What does that mean?**

    Experiencing him is that whatever work you are doing should be done with love, whether you are doing your household chores or meeting friends. Where there is love, there is Sai. Steer clear of negative thoughts.

    A few minutes of invocation in the morning when you wake up will help you through the day. Sit in silence, shut your eyes and visualize Sai in front of you, think of your Guru, your Mother, your Father and seek their guidance. You can then talk to Sai and tell him what you feel. Learn to listen to him. You can converse with Sai, throughout the day too.

9. **How do I shun negativity from my life?**

   To drive negativity away, one needs to be extremely positive. Negativity drains you and pulls you away from your life's purpose. To steer away from negativity, focus on the good things that come across your way. Read books that help you to be positive. Surround yourself with people who are positive and help you grow spiritually.

10. **What if I am attacked by negative feelings and negative people?**

    Sprinkle consecrated water and apply Sai's udi/ash. Read holy scriptures and consume the blessed water. Scriptures have the power to ward off negativity from your mind.

11. **Is that enough?**

    It is a shield that will act as a barrier and prevent negative forces from attacking you.

12. **How often should I apply udi?**

    When you wake up and when you step out of your home.

13. **What are negative forces?**

    Negative forces exist in the form of greed, anger, hatred, pride, envy, lust....

    These negative forces will prevent you from growing to your full potential. They don't want you to recognise your true self, thus they drain you, they entice you with Maya to keep you away from positivity. To safeguard yourself you need to be disciplined.

14. **Isn't life all about enjoying the materialistic pleasures bestowed on us?**

    One should enjoy materialistic pleasures, but without attaching oneself to them. The materialistic comforts you have earned should not become a reason for attachment to this world. Comforts are but frills in your life, your true goal should never be forgotten.

15. **How do I know what is my goal?**

    When you begin a dialogue with Sai or your deity or Master you will learn of your goal. When your faith in Sai increases you will yourself walk towards the goal. His invisible hand will lead you. Be patient, even if you cannot hear him. If you keep your faith, he will hold your hand and walk you.

16. **Who is Sai?**

    Sai is a powerful energy, a part of the divine that stays in the earth realm to protect and guide souls. Sai is pure light. We are all a speck of that light. When you utter *Allah Maalik*, you are reminding your consciousness that you are but a part of that effulgent light that needs to shake the dust it has collected since life times. God is the Supreme Power and Sai a true Sadhguru.

17. **I wish to see Sai.**

    To see Sai all you need is Faith. Faith can move mountains. If you sincerely desire, he will talk to you. If your faith is strong, your love is pure he will not negate your prayers. For he loves you more than you love him. Sai's devotees are spread all around the world. Even those who have never visited Shirdi have experienced his presence in their lives.

18. **Where does my soul want to go?**

    Ask yourself this question where do I want to go? The Universe is vast, in this vastness you are but a speck and you have a role to play. Are you playing that role? How would you know what is your reason to take birth in this planet at this time? Start by taking time out to pray, to connect. Connection to self is the key. When you connect to your Higher Self your energy vibrates at a higher level. To raise your consciousness, begin everyday by sitting for a few minutes in silence. Pray to Sai for his guidance, Sai is ever pervading, ever generous.

19. **How will I be successful?**

    Success is measured in different ways. For some success is material gains, for some it's about finding an emotional balance, for some it is all about power and wealth. There are those who feel successful by putting others down and feeling superior to them.

    In reality success is a measure of how much self-worth and peace you have attained. Do you love yourself enough? Are you peaceful? Is your conscience clear. Only when you understand the true self will you find success. Don't look for it in the outside world.

    You are successful when you have been instrumental in spreading joy to others. Don't run after material gains, make your life pure and simple.

20. **Life is difficult, how do I handle my problems?**

    If there is no darkness, how would you know light. If there are no problems, then how will you understand and evolve in life? Souls come to this earth for a reason. They are here to evolve and learn lessons. You chose to experience this human birth. It is in these experiences that your soul finds its true self.

To handle your problems, you need to believe first that you are not this body, you are but playing your part as this body. Detach yourself from the hurdles you face, believe them to be a learning. Learn the lesson and move on. When suffering is beyond your control and you find it difficult to overcome, calling upon Sai will help. For Sai will hold your hand and guide you through and at times he will take your suffering upon himself.

At this moment in time Sai has appointed many healers around the world to bring relief to those souls that are unable to come out of their suffering.

21. **How do I dedicate my life to Sai?**

    You need to do your duty, serve the needy, don't be greedy. Be happy with what you receive. Sai does not want silver or gold to be showered upon him, all He asks is that you talk to Him, treat Him as your family and you will feel His presence. Let Him guide you towards the Light.

22. **Can I find happiness in work and duty?**

    Happiness is within you. Whether you are at your job or doing your household chores. The key to remaining happy is in believing that whatever you are doing you are placing it at Sai's feet. Leave your day's work, struggles and sorrows at his feet. Do your work diligently and leave the rest to him.

23. **Why should I believe in Sai?**

    Even if you don't believe, Sai is with you. Even if you don't see air, you cannot survive without breathing it. The life you are living is because of *prana*. You cannot see *Prana*, but it is a reality. When the veil of illusion is eliminated, you will feel and see him. If you believe in any other form that is guiding you to the Truth, that too is Sai.

24. **What are the consequences of not praying?**

What are the consequences of not eating? You may last for a while, but with time you become physically feeble. Similarly you may not realize it but without prayers your soul blurs. It needs fuel to revive itself and that can happen with prayers.

Prayers are the steps that lead you to the Eternal Truth. Prayer is the means to attain salvation. Prayer is your cane. Prayer is the mode of communication to the All-Pervading God.

25. **I feel sad and depressed at times. I am lost at times.**

Depression is a serious issue facing this generation. Overdose of social media, gadgets and the need for validation from the world has destroyed this generation. People are seeking happiness in the outside world, when in reality all they need to do is turn inward.

They have to understand that the power is within them. Happiness and peace are attained by looking inward. I would like to tell the young minds to be strong.

If you are not strong from within, then you will always be insecure and restless in the outside world. When you connect within and talk to ME, you will experience true joy and will never feel alone.

Stop looking for acceptance in the outside world, seek it within. You will experience miracles in your life. Through these miracles you will understand the Truth about Sai. Have faith in Sai and let his grace pour. Let Sai hold your hand and guide you towards self-realization.

26. **What is it that Sai wishes of his devotees?**

All that Sai wants is that his devotees evolve in this birth to avoid the continuous cycle of life and death. Only when the soul evolves, will he be in search of Truth.

Many a devotee lose their faith in certain births and despite Sai's many indications they pay no heed. They backtrack in their growth and are unable to find the right path. When Sai feels it is the right time, He nudges his devotees to walk the path they are destined to. At times devotees listen and at times they ignore His teachings.

Sai lets those bhaktas be, silently watching them as they move on in their journey. Self-realization is not achieved by paying for a few courses, it is achieved with the mercy of a true guru. In this era of *kaliyug*, there are many a so called gurus awaiting to fleece you of your wealth and in return give quarter cent of knowledge that will take you nowhere. Sai wants you to be careful of such Masters. A true guru guides you to the Truth without taking a penny for his service.

If you have never known of Sai, now is the time to shut your eyes and think of Him. He will be there with you, blessing you. Sai is the real *Sadhguru*. Bow at His feet. At His feet you will find the merging of the sacred rivers. At His feet are the *tirths* (holy places) of the world, at His feet you will find true peace.

27. **Who to believe and who not to?**

At times devotees have questions about these so-called gurus. Many seekers have been cheated by fake gurus. But don't lose hope, there are many true Masters at this time on the plane. If you are truly searching for one, he will find you. Don't lose heart if you have been swindled. Consider it as paying off your karmas.

28. **What if I desire something, will I get?**

Remember desire is what keeps you bonded to the cycle of life and death. Your desire should not be a command but a supplication to the Supreme Power that this is my desire but only if you feel it is right for me, bless me with it. Leave your desires at the feet of Sai and let him decide if you deserve it or not.

29. **How do I go about my day?**

    Each one has their routine and situations. But the best way to start your day is taking out time in the early morning to connect to your inner self. When you wake up think of Sai, when you sleep think of Sai. Through the day do your *nama japa*, Sai should dominate your thoughts. For when you do so you will automatically forego of any kind of behaviour that would disturb your peace of mind. Negative thoughts will steer clear from you.

30. **What to do when angry?**

    First of all, why should you get angry? When you are angry your heart pumps harder. Instead of getting angry, speak firmly to get your work done not rudely.

    Irritation and frustration lead to anger. To avoid being irritated breathe deeply before you respond and chant the name of Sai. Observe the situation as if you were an outsider. Then respond to the situation.

31. **How can I spread joy?**

    Joy is spread by your thoughts and actions. When you spread happiness by controlling your mood swings, the atmosphere around you will be joyous. Light a candle everyday by your altar or wherever you are working.

    Help those who come to you, if you cannot do so financially then do so with emotional support. Don't ridicule anyone and be compassionate to all, especially to birds and animals. A calm mind vibrates joy without any effort. Be calm.

32. **Why should I pray?**

    Pray for your evolvement, pray for the Universe to evolve, pray for your loved ones. Prayer is the only way to attain the Truth. Otherwise you will remain in the clutches of delusion that is Maya.

33. **Why was Maya created?**

    Maya is an illusion there is no other reason for its creation, except that Maya is instrumental in teaching us lessons. A teacher, who ties your eyes and lets you see beautiful dreams. Her job is to keep you enticed so that you never think of untying the cloth and seeing the Truth.

34. **How should I pray?**

    A prayer invocating THE DIVINE, YOUR MASTER, YOUR PARENTS. Pray for the up liftment of humanity. Pray for peace on earth. Send love to Mother Earth.

    After which you should do whatever your Master had guided you to do. When you have followed that through your day converse with Sai.

    Seek his guidance in whatever you are doing. In doing so you are connecting to your Higher Self. Your Higher Self is in direct communication with your Sai, the Universe, or who so ever you wish to call upon. That source that is Pure Light.

35. **How should I improve myself as a human being?**

    Improvement comes with a determination to change. Chalk out the areas you wish to improve in. Be aware of your flaws and work on them with determination and see the change.

36. **How do I choose my friends?**

    Wisely.
    If you don't have the wisdom to distinguish,

connect to your inner self and observe the feelings you have when this person is around. No one is bad. It is your bondage with them that creates animosity or love. If there is no bondage there will be neutrality. If there is a good bondage you will work in tandem and if there has been a bad past connection, then there will be conflicts.

Whatever it is, you need to remind yourself that the one with whom you have disputes are the ones who are here to teach certain lessons. Learn them without attaching yourself to the person. Once you have learnt your lesson they will move on. Do not carry forward any baggage. The moment you ponder, discuss and rack your brain, the bondage will carry forward to your next birth. Regarding the ones that work with you in tandem, they too will be there as per your karmic requirement.

37. **How do I know what lessons I am here to learn?**

    You may not know them consciously, but your subconscious mind is aware. Go with the flow, awareness will set in.

38. **Why are we here?**

    Because you chose to be here.

39. **Where is the Supreme Power?**

    Everywhere.

40. **Where is Sai?**

    Sai is in all and all are in Sai.

    'My devotees deviate from their path at times. They are not sure which direction they wish to go. Unable to understand what is coming their way and what they are asking for. Sometimes I give them what I know they will require. It is not always about materialistic gains. It is also about spiritual gain that will help wash away their past sins.' Shirdi Sai Baba

41. What does Sai gain?

'I gain the love of my devotees. Their ego is slashed with my love. They think positive and their mind is focussed on the Supreme Power.'

42. Where does one find you?

'I am everywhere. I am in the hearts and souls of my devotees.'

43. Why do bhaktas many a times fail to recognize you when you come face to face?

'It is part of my *leela*. I test their faith so that they don't slack in their devotion. I am there, yet they cannot see me. 'I can see that their mind and heart are arguing. But there will come a time, when there will be no conflict within and they will recognize Me.'

44. Why do you play such leelas dear Sai?

'These *leelas* are the ones mother's play with their children, siblings with each other, friends play with their friends. For I am another you.'

45. How do I crush my ego?

'There is no ego if there is no ME.'

46. How to say there is no ME?

'By loving your Sai so much that there is no difference between YOU and ME. Fill your heart with love and all you will see is your SAI.'

47. How to find the true self?

True self is the purest form of bliss. To find your true self you need to live a simple pure life. It may sound difficult at first but once you start living that kind of life, everything will fall into place easily. Introspection, is vital. When you sit with yourself and acknowledge the real you, you will find it easier to move ahead with your spiritual practises.

Beware of wrong energies. There will be energies that will interfere in your practise. These energies wish to act as a barrier between you and your true self. It is these energies that make you deviate, so learn to shun them. Anger, hatred, lust, jealousy, pride and greed, these are your enemies.

48. **What are the components of this life?**

The five elements of this life are Fire, Water, Earth, Air and Space.

49. **What is Prana?**

Prana is life force, it's energy. Prana and air are interconnected although not the same. You can increase this prana, through meditation. When your attention is one pointed your pranas, your life force increases. That is the reason meditation brings a glow to one's face and makes them active.

What is it that truly makes you happy? What is it that you want out of your life? What is your purpose? These are some of the questions that souls who have overcome material attachment begin asking themselves. It is by meditating that these answers surface. Your energy force is vibrant. Negativity will try to distract you, be alert. Clean your space, open windows and doors for sunlight to enter. The sun has powerful rays that will clear the negative space at your home.

Signs of negativity: Depression, irritation, anger, laziness, drowsiness, overweight.

Beware of these signs. Now you may ask if there is a Supreme Power, deities and saints then how is it that negative energies take control? To that my simple answer is; Advaita, Duality. To understand light, you need to experience darkness. To value the goodness in life you need to have obstacles.

50. **Why does God let negative energies persist?**

    God does not interfere. He only spreads light so that the negativity diminishes. In darkness all that you need is a flame. God is the Supreme Light and from this light have emerged powerful souls and other souls who have given in to their inner demons. It is those powerful souls who guide these lost souls and help them return Home.

51. **What should one do to steer clear of falling into negativity?**

    Simply steer clear by being focussed and connected to Sai.

52. **Is there a constant battle between the positive and the negative?**

    Yes, there is a constant battle and it is the positive that usually wins.

53. **What is it humans should do to save themselves from Nature's fury?**

    Respect and nurture it. Stop destroying what is not yours. Control your greed and consume as much as required. Don't overfeed yourself. If you don't over consume than your requirement, there will be abundance on Earth.

54. **What is human reality?**

    Humans are divine that is your reality. But at present that divinity is obscured by greed and hatred.

55. **How to recognize karma?**

    For every action there is a reaction. That reaction is karma. How you react to a situation is your karma. Reactions can be with your thoughts, words and deeds. React positively, think positive, speak positive. And you will only gain positivity in your life. If you have to bear the pain of a past karma, bear it with a smile. Don't react in a negative manner. Accept and move on. Think of the now. Live happily now.

56. **Good or bad? How do I decide?**

    With goodness energy levels rise. With wrong habits, your energy dissipates.

57. **Who is an ideal partner?**

    If you expect your partner to be ideal or you expect your children to be ideal then make sure you have changed yourself primarily.

58. **Will the world end?**

    The world will not end, your ego will be crushed.

59. **An ideal life.**

    A life dedicated to self-growth and growth of others. Living with joy and spreading joy.

    Kindness in every word and deed. Compassion towards all.

60. **Judging others.**

    Judging others and putting them down is a sin. A sin that will add to your karmic account. Never criticize or make fun of anyone. Neither in thoughts nor words nor actions.

61. **Idealism?**

Being Ideal is but a word that adds pressure to your existence. Each one is a product of their *gunas*, their *samskaras* and their purpose in life. If you see everyone the way you see yourself, you will find that whether they are ideal or not, you love them for who they are.

62. **Measuring one's self-worth.**

This world has reached a stage where self-worth is being measured with likes on social media. It is adding pressure on youngsters to perform their best, look their best. Is it physically, emotionally, mentally, socially possible, to excel everytime? You should not be dependent on others for your self-worth. When you are looking for appreciation from others and do not receive it, you slip into depression. Those moments of weakness and lack of self-worth is driving many a people to commit suicide.

A dose of spirituality in the education system will go a long way in bringing up confident and happy children. It is important for youngsters to understand that their soul has taken birth for a reason, it is here to evolve. They are not the body that they have been born with, but a soul. Teaching of this concept is a must in schools. *Kaliyug* has brought about a fall in human race. Instantaneous results will be noticed in these times, so measure every step that you take.

63. **Soul searching.**

There are many questions that humans have towards life and in desperation they end up paying large sums to teachers who themselves are yet to evolve. See the intent of the person and his commitment towards the Truth.

64. **Why is devotional bhakti in kaliyug so significant?**

    In this yuga the bhakti that will bring you close to the Supreme Power is chanting of His name with devotion. Not a mechanical recitation but a recitation that is filled with pure love.

65. **What do you do with devotees who have lost their path?**

    I let them be. They will come around.

66. **What if your devotees are taking wrong actions?**

    I scold them, at times I explain them and at times. I let them learn the lessons that they are meant to learn.

67. **What if both the devotees in a battle are your bhaktas?**

    That happens all the time. How can I take sides? I bless both my devotees to learn their lessons. It is their past life bondage that makes them do whatever they do. At times I intervene and cut the cords for good, eliminating their prior bondage. At times my bhaktas have to work out their bondages through forgiveness.

68. **Are there devotees who you love more than others?**

    I love them all equally. Rich or poor, big or small. I see no difference.

69. **What is true joy?**

    True joy is but peace of mind. Peace of mind is attained by connecting within. When you connect with your Higher self you will experience true ecstasy.

70. **What is it that Sai wishes to tell his devotees, his children?**

    'Don't be disheartened when your path is filled with obstacles. Have faith and call out to Me.'

71. **When should I come to Shirdi?**

    When I call you. When you hear a voice nudging you that it is time to visit Shirdi. If you do come, make sure you come with a clean slate. Don't judge nor criticize your surroundings. Come with joy and leave in ecstasy.

72. **My life is a maze; I am lost at times.**

    It is in those books that I have guided, will you find your answers. Read them consistently.

73. **Is Shirdi the only tirath sthaan (holy place) where I can find you?**

    Shirdi is where my bones are laid but wherever my devotees have placed me with love and devotion, whether in the form of an idol or a picture I am there.

74. **How can I help the needy?**

    Help them not only with *annadaan* (charity of food) but also *gyaan* (knowledge).

75. **How does one know that a certain relationship is toxic?**

    Where there is no love, only criticism, where words flow in the form of lava. Where violence is inflicted, such a relationship is toxic.

76. **What should one do under such circumstances?**

    If one can move away without causing much pain, they should move on. But when one is duty bound and has no way to come out then prayers is the only way out. Prayers will bring a change and the toxicity in the relationship will disappear.

77. **What if they don't change?**

    If you have faith in Sai and pray wholeheartedly there will be change. Change that will begin with you. Your positivity will be so infectious that it will bring a change in the other person.

78. **Why some relationships last forever and some ties are cut off?**

    Relationships last and get cut off as per karmic bondage. Also, how you react in moments of discord. If you are patient then your relations will last longer. But if both parties concerned are impatient then the relationship dies. At times it gets further entangled and in the next birth they come back and start a relationship that is filled with hatred and enmity. That is why it is imperative that you don't attach yourself to such relationships. Be cordial, be patient and detach yourself. Don't criticise or judge that relationship. Let time take its course.

79. **What is penance in this yug?**

    In *kaliyug* true penance is prayer. Prayers to the Supreme Power. Chanting of his name constantly.

80. **Then why do we pray to other deities? Shouldn't we pray only to the Supreme Father?**

    When you pray to deities or saints your prayers reach faster to the Supreme Father. It is like express mail.

81. **If we merge into the Supreme, we will lose ourselves.**

    In losing yourself you will find Him. As the river merges with the ocean you will merge into the vastness of the Supreme Power.

82. **Should I listen to my inner voice?**

    Your inner voice is your Higher Self. And your Higher Self is All pervading. Connect to your inner voice and you will be connected to Me.

83. **Will the world come to an end?**

    End is a new beginning. The world will not end but what will end is human greed, pride, anger, lust and hatred.

84. **How should I save Mother Earth?**

 Mother Earth can be saved if you change your ways. Put an end to your greed. Keep your wants minimum. This pandemic has hopefully taught you that one can survive with minimum. So why this constant desire for accumulation? Change yourself before it's too late. Greed has no limit, so control it before it destroys the Earth.

85. **Is Mother Earth furious?**

 A Mother's anger never lasts if you seek forgiveness. Similarly, Mother Earth is agitated at this moment. She can be calmed if you promise a change. Work on that change and keep your greed in control. Don't abuse your power over the earth. Don't destroy forests and kill innocent animals.

86. **Why do we fear suffering?**

 You fear suffering because you get attached to this body. When you learn to accept that suffering is but temporary, you will be able to endure the pain. Suffering does not last forever nor does joy. Those who are balanced in happiness and sorrow are truly peaceful.

87. **How does one detach from pain? It is so difficult when someone is in physical pain.**

 It is not easy to detach but with constant meditation and prayers comes Faith. When your faith in Sai is strong you will accept suffering and pain as part of your karmic cycle. If suffering comes, accept it as Sai's grace.

88. **Sai, it's not so easy to endure pain.**

 Life is not always a bed of roses, there will be thorns. It's these thorns that protect the rose. It is in this suffering that you will find yourself evolving. For you would have learnt to accept pain and pleasure.

89. **Help me understand this better Sai.**

It's very simple. When you walk a path without hurdles, life is easy. A rocky path will be filled with obstacles and the journey exhausting but every challenge you will face on this path will make your faith stronger.

Souls make a choice before they are born. A straight road is very rarely chosen for it does not satisfy the soul's requisition. There are no lessons learnt. But when the road is curvy and rocky, lessons of endurance, patience and other latent qualities emerge. Think of life as a play and play your part well.

90. **Why do we suffer?**

Suffering is a part of your birth plan. Without suffering you will not be able to learn any lessons.

91. **Do you help your bhaktas cut their karmas Sai?**

If I had to show you the list of your bondages you would be unable to fathom the fact of how entangled your karma is, at times I intervene to untangle a few threads so that your journey is easier.

92. **How to recognise your grace?**

You will feel my presence in your life in everything that you do. It is then you must understand that you are blessed.

93. **I cannot meditate.**

If you cannot meditate then talk to Me, sit with Me. Read the *Satcharitra* or any holy book. Don't get frustrated if you cannot meditate. What is more important is that you connect to your Higher self.

94. **I want to do good but don't know how.**

Doing good is the easiest. Do to others what you wish for them to do. Talk to others as you want them to talk to you. Wish for others what you wish for yourself. Goodness will follow.

95. **I don't have a good voice to sing to you.**

    It does not matter how you sing what matters is with what *bhav* (intention) you sing. I only feel your love. Music is a form of the Divine and when you sing, you are connecting yourself to the vibrations of the Divine. It is those vibrations that reach my ears.

96. **I want to always be at your feet.**

    If I am in your heart then you don't have to worry about my feet.

97. **What were the reasons that made Sai upset? Why would he bombard his devotees at times?**

    The reason Sai did what he did was to protect his devotees from the evil energy that they brought along with them. At times Sai would be upset with his devotee's incapability to follow the principles of life.

    Sai did not like his devotees wasting their time in condoning and criticising others. He wanted his bhaktas to spend their time wisely. He would be upset on some occasions for reasons that are incomprehensible to human mind. Sai would take the sufferings of his bhaktas. His body had the ability to take all the pain but at times the pain would be unbearable and yet he would smile through it.

    Don't judge Sai for his outer appearance or his display of anger for he was a man of God. It is Sai who is protecting his devotees from the clutches of evilness and is a saviour. Bow down to Sai for it is He who is protecting the Universe.

98. **Is it okay if I don't take out time to pray but do good deeds.**

    Prayers are not mechanical. Helping and sharing are prayers. Caring and serving others are prayers. Living a modest life is a prayer. Kindness and compassion towards others is prayer.

If your life is a prayer you don't need to take out time. You are living your prayer every moment.

99. **How do I raise my consciousness?**

By constant practise of sitting in silence. With one pointed attention on Sai.

100. **What is it that I need to do to get away from my fears?**

Your fears are a creation of your mind. When you have controlled your mind, your fears too will disappear. Surrender yourself at the feet of Sai, there will be no fear.

Sai's Guidance in Marriages and Relationships

101. **In a marriage how should the couple behave with each other?**

The announcement of their relationship as husband and wife brings the grace of the deities. For it is this relationship that furthers the growth of the Universe. It is in this union that another soul finds their way to earth.

Couples take vows of love, forgiveness, acceptance and an eternal promise to be with each other through thick and thin. They should comply with those vows and not allow their ego to come between them. There should be pure divine love for each other with acceptance of each other's flaws.

102. **What happens when that relationship breaks off?**

If couples decide to break their relationship, they should do so amicably. There should be no slander nor the desire for revenge.

Marriage is a sacred reunion of two souls, souls that have accepted each other and if they decide to break that relationship that has been blessed by deities, they should do so with cordial agreement.

Patience is key for a relationship to survive. And if one partner is weak, the other has to be extra strong to hold the marriage together.

103. **What happens when one partner cheats?**

The person who breaks the sacred vows, will have to bear dire consequences. For births the sinner will come back to learn this lesson.

At times the lesson is learnt in this birth through a series of illness and mental issues or in their future births they are cheated upon by their partner.

104. **How to keep one's marriage afloat when there are multitude of issues?**

The only way to keep a marriage afloat is through patience. Even if one partner in the marriage is understanding and patient, the marriage will last. But if both the partners are on logger heads and incapable of controlling their irritation and anger, their reactions will only lead to further bondage.

105. **A model wife.**

A model wife is a mirror to a model husband. Not only a wife but a man too has to be a model husband. Model man or wife is a creation of the mind. It is a mental list of expectations from your partner.

Instead make a mental list of how you should be the perfect husband or wife. How you could bring happiness in your partner's life.

106. **How should one choose their partner?**

    Sometimes souls have chosen their partner before they take birth. As they choose their parents, they are given a choice of partner too. The human mind has no memory of that decision and at times makes the wrong decision on the physical plane.

    Don't choose your partner on the basis of physical appearance only. Your partner should be a companion and a teacher. Let your inner voice guide you to your chosen soul.

107. **Is marriage an all for a human.**

    Marriage is the most joked and revered institution. Humans tend to regret their choice after a few years. Marriage is a union of two souls who have come down to add their bit to the Universe. The purity of a relationship elevates you to a higher level of spirituality. It is this sacred union that creates a new life and it is in those moments that you touch the surface of the spiritual plane. It is an ecstatic moment that is celebrated, in the purest form of love.

108. **Is it true that married couples come back as couples for many births?**

    Marriages may not be for births but relationship between two souls continue till their karmic accounts are settled.

Pearls of Wisdom

*In the following pages
Sai has communicated 108 messages.
Messages that have deep meaning.*

Fold your hands in prayer, bow at his feet and seek his grace. It is not in diamonds and jewels but in simplicity and humility that you will find Sai. Shut your eyes and think of Shirdi Sai Baba. Let his image be your centre point. Focus on his feet there is a message for you.

Think of a number between 1-108

*May His words resonate with you, for in his words there is power, in his words are hidden messages.
In his words you will find peace and happiness.*

1. Humans tend to lose faith when life does not give them what they wish for. They then grumble, argue and fight with their loved ones. Remember, nothing comes in life to you if you don't deserve it. When you spread joy, you are bound to receive joy. God is merciful. By constantly complaining you are destroying your good karmas.

2. Trust in the power of the Supreme, trust in his grace. Trust that Sai will guide and protect you. Do not despair if things don't turn out to be as you expected. There is always a reason when they don't.

3. Every human is a product of his/her own doing. Don't take life for granted. Work on yourself. Work towards being a better human being. Do good to others and good will come back to you. Help the needy.

4. Be firm in your belief. Don't take any wrong action in moments of despair. Sai will help you cross hurdles that come your way. Be strong. Have faith that Sai is always with you, watching you, guiding you.

5. Many a thought, many a choice, many conflicts. Life if full of illusions, that pull you away from your goal. To free yourself from it, take the name of Sai with faith and you will find the forked roads merge into one. Don't let yourself be overpowered by the influence of Maya.

6. Seek not only joys and pleasures, seek the feet of Sai. Seek his service and seek His blessings. Don't let yourself be carried away by materialistic pleasures.

7. Nature helps heal negativity. When in doubt or when you are confused, spend time in open spaces. Pay attention to the chirping of birds. In the vastness of Nature, remind yourself of the gifts that the Universe

has bestowed on you. Sit on the soil, connect to Mother Earth. She will heal you.

8. Don't let anyone pull you down and ridicule you. Don't take it in your stride. Stand up and fight for justice. War of words is not the way, you can win evil with purity and patience.

9. Don't force others to do what you wish for them to do. Don't ridicule others for their weaknesses. Work on yourself and correct your flaws. Each one has their own lessons to learn. You can only guide, but don't punish them for their errors.

10. Mocking and shaming are but traits of those who lack self-confidence. When you shame or mock anyone, you are sucking into their negativity. If you mock and shame others, you will not be spared by the law of karma. Watch your thoughts, words and action.

11. It is your 'I' that is the reason for your distance between You and Sai. Your 'I' will only bring misery. When you let go off your 'I' and merge with Sai you will find true happiness and peace.

12. Silence is the prized possession of humans. In silence you can avert arguments and rows. When in doubt remain silent. When upset, remain silent. God hears your silence, be assured.

13. Mind the mind for if you don't, your mind will take you for a ride. It is this mind that takes you towards the Light or leads you to Darkness. Train your mind with one pointed devotion to Sai.

14. When a thousand thoughts cross your mind and you are unable to still them, let them be. Don't fuel those thoughts. Be an observer and observe. Detach yourself from it and they will slowly disappear.

15. Home is where the heart is and a home that is filled with love is the abode of God. A negative atmosphere at home will destroy your peace. Create a harmonious atmosphere at home. Be patient and understanding with your family members.

16. Don't let the feelings and actions of others affect your mind. Don't be agitated if someone is bickering and gossiping about you. That would be their karma. Your karma is to protect yourself. Chant the name of Sai and you will be shielded from negative people.

17. Discard away from your life all that pulls you down. Relations, friends and acquaintances that disturb your peace of mind. If you need to cut ties, do so amicably. Don't hurt anyone in the bargain, be careful. Do your duty without attaching yourself to the results.

18. Those friendships that help you evolve are worth keeping. Cut ties with those that lead you towards the wrong path. Stay away from those who pull you down. If you have to walk alone, do so. Don't forget that it is better to be alone than to be with those that deviate you from your goal. Choose your friends wisely.

19. Repeating Sai's name mechanically will not draw you closer to Him. Call out to Sai with love and He will be there for you. Let go off your ego and you will find Sai by your side.

20. Thinking and over thinking will not help solve your problems. Every problem has a solution. You need to delve deep within to find it. Chant the name of Sai with devotion and you will find answers to your problems.

21. Don't measure your success with material gains. True success is not in the wealth you have accumulated but in finding your True Self and recognising the Divine powers that are within you.

22. Don't be stuck in the rigmarole of life. Experience and enjoy the beauty around you. Take time out to be with yourself. Spend time in Nature. Talk to the birds and trees, listen to the oceans and brooks. In the vast oceans there is wealth of wisdom, in the skies are the secrets of the Universe.

23. Difficulties will come your way. Happiness and sorrow are part of life. Don't fret when difficult times take your peace away. Every hurdle is a lesson, every problem has a solution. Soon like a diamond you will shine.

24. When your boat rocks and you have nowhere to go, place your head at Sai's feet and surrender. Faith moves mountains, you will soon see your sorrows disappear.

25. Cleanse yourself with the name of the Lord. Cleanse, cleanse, cleanse till you shine bright like a diamond and merge with the Supreme.

26. Patience and Faith will take you a long way. It is these treasures that you must use abundantly. Don't be irritated if things don't go your way. Believe that Sai has something better for you in store, go with the flow.

27. Sever the demons that are inside you. Cut off relations with those that misguide you. Don't allow evil to control you. Desires give rise to anger. Control your desires.

28. Live with love and humility, compassion and strength. Let go of your pride and surrender at His feet.

29. Don't despair when sorrow comes knocking at your door. Let the wave of pain rise. Soon it will subside, nothing stays forever. Let not the mind tell you otherwise. With Patience and Faith you will overcome your pain.

30. Challenges are part of life. Don't let challenges scare you. If there is a challenge accept it with the belief that Sai will take care of you. It does not matter if you fail, for you would have tried.

31. Selfish gains will not take you anywhere. It is but a short-term reward. If you want to ask Sai for anything, ask for spiritual growth.

32. Be not the person who breaks others heart. Instead be the one who mends hearts with kind words. In small joys you will find true peace.

33. Let not others berate you, let not anyone crush your dreams. Allow not injustice and don't ever bend in front of those who take advantage of you. Fear not those who wish to harm you, for Sai shields you with Light.

34. Mind your own business, don't try to judge others and find faults in them. There is enough of your own dirt to be cleansed. Mind your thoughts, words and deeds and walk towards the path of self-realization.

35. In the scheme of things of the Universe you are but a speck. Shun your ego, be humble and disciplined. Nothing is yours on this Earth. Everything belongs to the Supreme.

36. In the name of religion, you kill and hate. In the name of religion, wars break. Why don't humans realize that religion is but man made? Love is the true religion. Sai has shown the path, yet you sway.

37. Shine bright with your actions, do good deeds. Opportunities come your way. It is up to you to take or leave them. If you have a clear mind, you will take a right decision. Your soul longs to be at the feet of the Supreme.

38. Value Time for time never comes back. Live in the present. Let bygones be bygones. Don't attach yourself to the past. In equanimity you will find solace.

39. Sing to Sai, sit by His feet and open your heart, let the tears flow as you sing to Him in devotion. Connect to your Sai Baba, let not the outer world distract you.

40. Be sure of what you want. Have faith and ask not for material gains. Material gains only entangle you further into the cycles of birth and death. Freedom is attained when you have nothing left to seek, except devotion. In humility you will find your answers.

41. Thinking negative thoughts, attracts negativity into your life. Positive thoughts will clear your mind and detach you from all that bogs you down. If you live in fear, you will never find Truth.

42. Mind is a double-edged sword. If you don't control it, it will take you for a ride. Tame your mind through meditation and prayers. Wake up early and spend time with yourself.

43. Don't allow yourself to be consumed by hatred. Don't allow yourself to be inflated with pride. Remember that you are a spark from the Divine. Spread joy.

44. Sai is your best friend and guide who can help you walk through life. Hold His hand and let Him walk you through your difficult time. Surrender at Sai's feet, let go of your pride.

45. Amidst the turmoil around you, find shelter within. When you do so you will find peace. Go within every day and sit by yourself. Leave your worries at His feet.

46. When in doubt remind yourself of the unconditional love of Sai. Don't let your ego intervene. Don't let doubt veil your faith. You believe yourself to be intelligent but the truth is that without His mercy you are nothing.

47. If life was a bed of roses would you have thought of Sai? Accept the hurdles that come your way. Think not of what you don't have, instead think of what you have. Accept His grace.

48. Let your mind be free of worries. When you worry too much, your health is affected. When your mind is hopping from one worrisome thought to another bring it to attention by meditating on Sai. Chant His name.

49. Your mind is your friend and your enemy. At times it can lead you to the right path and at times it may force you to take wrong decisions. Before you make any decision think of Sai and ask for His guidance.

50. Not for fame nor for success, nor for material gains or wealth. If you raise your hands in prayer, do so for self-realization.

51. Don't let your ego take you for a ride. You may walk the path of spirituality but if your walk is filled with pride then you can never attain Liberation.

52. Don't worry about what people think of you. Mind not what he said or she said. Listen to the teachings of Sai, in them you will find true nectar. Go within and contemplate on your true Nature.

53. Raise not your voice on those who are meek. Raise not your hand on those who are unable to defend themselves. Be kind and compassionate and raise your Consciousness.

54. I ask of you to pray, not for selfish reasons. But for peace on Earth. Respect the animals and birds. Don't kill them for your selfish reasons, don't misuse your power. Seek not thrills from destroying Nature and animals around. Be compassionate to all.

55. Nothing is yours on this Earth. Everything is but a creation of the Supreme. You are here as a visitor. Guard the treasures of Nature. Don't waste. Save and guide those around you too.

56. Are you doing your duty? Are you thinking good for others? Revisit your thoughts of the day and check if they are good, bad or neutral. Weed out bad thoughts. Think no evil.

57. Don't swell with pride for you are but a speck of dust. Those who walk with pride and look down upon the less fortunate, never find peace within. Let go of your ego and all that keeps you from connecting to Sai.

58. Mind your words before you speak. Mind your actions and deeds. Every action will have a reaction and every word spoken will come back to haunt you.

59. Think not I am the best. Everyone is from the same light. Some have accumulated dust with time while some shine bright. When you meditate, darkness will disappear and the cobwebs within will be cleared.

60. Darkness disappears with light. Evil can be eradicated by spreading love. Don't allow your inner devils to take over. Give up on your anger or your anger will destroy you.

61. Grief and sorrow will lessen, when you are in control of your emotions. Not by being indifferent but by understanding that nothing is permanent. Believe in Sai and surrender your worries at His feet.

62. When you sincerely call out to Sai, He answers your prayers. Not only to fulfil your desires but to lead you to the Truth. Be aware of what you do and let go of your ego.

63. Let not there be greed within, let there not be anger within. Control your desires that lead you astray. Let not darkness keep you away. Let go off your ego and you will understand the true essence of Sai. Fall at His feet, ask for forgiveness. Your life will change.

64. Don't harm or hurt anyone intentionally or unintentionally. Every thought, word and action have consequences. Go within and seek peace. Don't entangle yourself further. Cut the cords that bind you.

65. Don't waste your time, sleeping and lazing. Make every minute of your life worth living. Darkness leads you towards lethargy and fear. Seek Light as it will lead you to the Truth.

66. Let the world turn upside down, but you keep your Faith strong. In darkness a spark of light brings hope. In pain, blessings from Sai bring relief.

67. Know the truth of life through communication and prayers. Don't pray mechanically but with a clean heart. Ask not for wealth but for mental peace. Ask not for fame but for liberation. Ask not for success but for connection to the Supreme.

68. Don't let the wrong distract you, choose your friends wisely. Be with those who energise you. Be with those who bring out the best in you. Shun negativity. Think good and seek the Truth.

69. Look not for fault in others for you have many yourself. Change yourself first and you will find a change in others. Be kind to all and bow your head with humility.

70. Keep the flame of faith burning despite the odds that come your way. This is your test and you will sail through. The Light within you will ward the devils away.

71. If you allow others to interfere, how will you dive within? Take your own decisions and believe in the power of the Supreme. Surrender at His feet. He will take care.

72. Right or wrong is not for you to judge, don't waste your time thinking about others. Focus on your life and your work. Spend time in remembering Sai and His miracles.

73. Let not your mind wander. Surrender your 'I' and 'Me' at the feet of Sai. Surrender your pride and anger. Find true joy in helping others.

74. Look not for power nor fame these are but transient pleasures. Real happiness is in loving Sai and surrendering at His feet. At His feet you will find true pleasure.

75. Throw away your garb, you are but Consciousness. It is this Consciousness that you need to raise. Rise and elevate others around you. Praise and sing the glories of the Supreme.

76. Sai's mercy is on you. Your life will take a different direction soon and good will flow into your life. Sai is by your side. When Light enters, darkness will disappear.

77. Don't be saddened if life is tough, don't give up if things don't go your way. Surrender at His feet and His blessings will guide you through.

78. Give and you will receive. Be kind and you will be filled with abundance. Faith in Sai and you Master is vital. Your Faith will help you fight your vices.

79. Devotion and Love will bring you closer to God. Knowledge without wisdom is of no use. Almighty is your Father and Maa Kali, Mother Divine. Pray to them for Grace.

80. Joys and sorrows are part of life. Nothing is attained without His Grace. If you believe He is with you, you will surely see Him.

81. These obstacles are your tests. Overcome these and find the Truth. In finding yourself, you will attain self-realization.

82. Why seek attention from those who do not care for you. Instead seek the blessings of Sai. If things do not go your way do not despair. Have faith and be calm. Sai will fill you with love and abundance.

83. Darkness is the absence of light. Ignorance is the absence of knowledge. Jealousy is the absence of self-confidence. Anger is but absence of self-love. It is these vices that you need to eliminate.

84. Accept what comes in your life, accept it with grace. In acceptance of your fate and through constant prayers will you find Heaven.

85. Don't make everything about yourself. Find joy in others happiness and help those in need. In helping others will you find God.

86. Let there be peace. Let there be love. Let there be happiness and compassion in this world. The more you pray, the closer you will find yourself to God.

87. Let the world turn upside down, you need to keep your Faith strong. Sai is with you at all times, there is no need to fear.

88. Take time out to meditate, take time out for prayers. Bow your head to the Almighty, seek His blessings. May your path be cleared of obstacles.

89. Think not what you don't have. Be grateful for what you have. It is in gratitude that you will find Sai.

90. Don't bend so much that you break your back. Stand up for yourself and fight the odds against you. Be strong. Sai is with you.

91. Not in this birth nor more to come will you find peace if you don't change from within. Cut the cords that bind you and let go off your greed.

92. Not in fear of Sai, but in love for Sai mend your ways and seek the Truth. Be aware of what you say and do. Let go off your ego and surrender at His feet.

93. True joy and peace are attained with prayers. Don't attach yourself to worldly affairs. Detach yourself and you will find peace.

94. Think not what you don't have, instead think of all that you have. Is it not enough that you have your Sai's love? Gaze at Him with love and devotion. Drop your ego, drop your fears. Sai will heal your pain.

95. Don't let yourself be consumed by hatred and pride. You are a part of the Divine plan. Realize it.

96. Why are you seeking attention from those who don't love you? Instead seek the feet of Sai where you will find true love in abundance.

97. Don't allow your mind to divert you from your goal. Don't allow your senses to keep you preoccupied with desires. Search for the Truth and work towards self-realization.

98. It is time to change yourself. In that change you will see a change in the world. Spread the name of Allah Malik. Surrender at HIS feet.

99. Believe in Sai. Believe in yourself. Do your duty with love and dedication. It does not matter if you are praised or not what matters is your honesty and integrity.

100. Respect and serve your parents. Fulfil your duties and give love. Help the old and sick who have no one to look after them. Doing so will cleanse you of your sins.

101. Not in friendships nor relations will you find fulfilment. It is only at His feet that you will find peace.

102. Don't think evil of anyone. Don't harm anyone. Every thought has a consequence. Don't let your mind wander hither and thither. Direct your mind towards the feet of Sai and let Him guide you through your life.

103. Discard those that disturb your peace of mind and do not let you shine. Discard those thoughts that trouble you and bring out the worst in you. Fill yourself with thoughts of the Divine.

104. Not in the valleys nor in the mountains, will you find peace. True peace is in remaining silent.

105. There will be obstacles in your life. Issues that will keep you preoccupied. Problems that will not let you raise your Consciousness. You have to work on yourself and cross these hurdles with Faith and Patience.

106. Calamities and disasters are wake up calls for Change. It is important to change yourself. Walk the path of spirituality and evolve. Pray to Sai for guidance.

107. You desire wealth, fame and success but you need to realize that these are impermanent. Only God's love is permanent.

108. When you put flowers at my feet. When you bathe Me and apply sandal paste on My forehead and dress Me. I am obliged to you forever.

Baba Hiral Shah

Baba Hiral Shah

Shirdi Sai Baba

Baba Hiral Shah and His Miracles

Baba Hiral Shah has left behind a legacy and his followers are spread all around the world, who serve at the aasthans of Sai Baba. Chownkis are held in these aasthans on every Thursday. Baba's disciples serve in these aasthans in some way or the other. It is the love and devotion towards Sai, that unites all the followers of Baba. Baba Hiral may not be physically present, but his essence is felt in every aasthan.

Sai loves his bhaktas,
Sai loves the Universe,
and the creatures that live in it.

He is Sai Baba,
He is Sai Maa,
He is Sai Sham,
He is Sai Ram,
He is Shiva,
He is Vishnu,
He is Brahma,
Call him by any name.
Think of him in any way, He will be there.

The following excerpt is by Roshini Mahtani who has been one of the closest disciples of Baba. Baba Hiral Shah loved all his devotees equally but there were few who dedicated their life to their Guru and Roshini is one of those enlightened souls. Always smiling and spreading joy Roshini provides assistance to the Sai aasthans around the world.

In the Laxmi Narayan temple in Mumbai, grains are provided every morning to the needy. On every festival along with the disciples even the poor are invited to the feast and are served by disciples themselves. Roshini with the support of her family and disciples of Baba works tirelessly to fulfil her Guru's dream of opening Sai aasthans for the benefit of human kind.

'It is in serving at the aasthans, that one's ego is crushed and humility surfaces.

It is in serving at the aasthans, that one learns to be disciplined.

It is in serving at the aasthans, that one learns to see everyone as equal.'

Baba Hiral Shah

My Guru Baba Hiral Shah
by Roshini Mahtani

My Baba Hiral Shah, that's how I would like to call him, not because the bond between us was the strongest, but because just the thought and the strong connection with him fills me with strength. It is from my Guru, that I derive the strength to fight the challenges that come my way, the faith of his presence and his protecting arms around me. My Guru gives me the strength to overcome grief, to withstand the disappointments and sadness that humanity is surrounded with.

Baba Hiral Shah has taught his followers to be positive and look for an opportunity even in problems. While the world thought of building on their wealth, Baba opened aasthans (temples) around the world for mankind.

They are called aasthans for the doors are open and everyone can serve, irrespective of caste or creed, name or position, religion or belief. Baba Hiral Shah was selfless and always placed his disciples even before his family. His teachings were many but what he most insisted on was, the importance of being a good human being, conducting oneself with dignity and love and not demeaning anyone.

Baba Hiral Shah worked for the betterment of mankind and his dream was to build as many aasthans as possible in the world. In an aasthan one has the luxury of sitting for hours and praying and there are no restrictions on timings. No one is forced to donate. Baba Hiral Shah has taught his disciples to converse with the Almighty and said that talking to the Supreme Power was the best form of prayer.

My Baba's journey was full of hardships and it was these hardships that guided him towards the path of spirituality. He was born in Yokohama, Japan to Mr. Choithram and Mrs. Parpati Mahtani. Baba was the only child and his mother left for heavenly abode when he was very young.

From being duped by his uncles, to doing a job in LIC, he experienced a lot of pain. But life became more difficult when his health did not support him and that's when someone advised him to visit the shrine of Baba Ashraf Khan in Ahmedabad. It was at the dargah of Baba Ashraf Khan, that Hiral Shah met Ammi Jaan, wife of the late saint. When Baba reached the dargah the first words that Ammi Jaan told him were that she had been waiting for him.

Ammi Jaan cured Hiral Shah and looked after him, as her son. Under her guidance and Baba Ashraf Khan's blessings Baba Hiral Shah walked on the path of spirituality and acquired powers to cure people. On his return to Mumbai, Baba Hiral Shah converted a part of his house into a temple. People started flocking to him on hearing about his miracles. Baba cured many a people and also solved their financial issues.

Seekers from all around the world visited Baba and experienced miracles in their life. The rich and poor stood at his door seeking his blessings and solutions to their problems. Whether it was for health, or a new venture or financial crisis or relationship issues; with Hiral Shah's blessings they would attain success in whatever they did. Their health would improve and their relationship issues would miraculously disappear.

Some would continue and follow his teachings but sadly there were some who would disappear once they had attained their materialistic goal. They would ignore Baba's teachings and never even return to thank him for helping them out. Hiral Shah always said to them don't thank me but do not forget Allah Malik, the Almighty who has answered your prayers.

Baba's teachings were many but some of the important lessons of life that he taught his disciples were:

The first one, be grateful in every situation no matter what you face whether happiness or sorrow, good or bad. Baba always told his disciples that they must look around them and they will understand that life has given thousands of reasons to be thankful for and the more one is grateful, more happiness will flow into their life.

The second lesson he always taught his disciples was to ask for forgiveness from Almighty. He always explained, that every problem, every sorrow that a man goes through is nothing but a result of his or her own karma. He would ask of his followers to raise their hands in prayer and seek forgiveness for those known and unknown sinful deeds that they have committed.

The third lesson Baba taught was that of introspection. He would ask his disciples to sit in silence and recollect their past mistakes and wrong decisions. He would ask his devotees to, 'sit in silence and your life will be revealed to you.'

The fourth lesson was the importance of a Guru. He said that every soul is answerable for their deeds and there is no one better than a Guru who can represent you in the court of the Almighty.

My Hiral Shah was more than a Guru to thousands of his disciples. He was a father to many, a friend to the young and old and a teacher to those who were in search of answers. Being with him was a blessing in itself. His aura was so powerful that being in his presence itself one's suffering would diminish.

Whosoever stepped in his aasthan was blessed. Parents who longed for a child were blessed with children, cancer patients were cured of their illness, those who could not walk, started walking. As I pen down his miracles it is very important to mention here how he even took his disciples karma on himself, healing them in return.

Baba said everyone has to face their Karmas, and the only one who can come between a person and his karma is a Guru, because a Guru is the only one who has the powers to control the impact of one's karma.

A Guru is the one who can reduce the effect of the karma so that a disciple does not have to suffer much. Baba would suffer many a times for the mistakes of his disciples. But he bore it all with a smile. He loved his disciple and remembered each one's name and recognised their voices immediately when they called him. He would bless not only the disciple who visited him but even the family of the disciple was protected by Baba.

Blessed are those, who found their Guru in My Hiral Shah because there was not a single day, when he did not raise his hands in prayers and seek blessings from The Almighty for all his disciples.

Baba Hiral Shah taught his followers the power of prayers. Prayers that could change one's destiny. Like Sai Baba, Baba Hiral Shah taught the importance of Faith and Patience. Many followers would find miracles just by sitting at his feet and resolving to walk the path towards Sai, towards the Truth. There were many questions raised by the doubtful minds. Minds that could not accept a family man becoming a Guru. Many criticized him, but Hiral Shah never got upset with anyone. He explained that running away to the Himalayas or wearing orange clothes did not guarantee self-realization or attaining the Truth. He believed that being in the society, fulfilling responsibilities and still being connected to the Almighty is the true challenge. The one who accepts these challenges to attain self-realization is a true devotee.

Baba lived a disciplined and simple life. He believed that greed was the root cause of all problems and one must control their greed. Baba's favourite meal was dal and roti and he kept his desire to bare minimum. A man of principles Baba spend his entire day helping people, listening to their problems and healing them personally. Many disciples called him everyday for blessing and those that lived abroad, he healed over the phone.

Baba like Sai Baba was compassionate and generous. He could never see anyone in pain and suffering and would go out of his way to help people emotionally and financially.

Baba preached on the importance of Light. He explained that with constant prayers one can keep away from darkness. Darkness that is evil. Evil here does not necessarily mean a demon who is physically harassing someone but they are the flaws within humans. Visiting aasthans, temples, gurudwaras, churches, mosque …..on a regular basis makes one positive. For these places of worship are filled with positive energies.

Baba believed in the power of music and said that it was the easiest way to connect to the Supreme Power. He encouraged devotional singing at aasthans. Baba himself danced joyously during the chownkis (kirtans) with his disciples whose faces would be filled with joy when they watched their Guru dancing along with them. He held their hands and each one felt loved and special when Baba danced with them. The vibrations of the aasthan during those times are so high that people are in a trance.

Chownkis are still held in all the aasthans and till today when the followers dance in joy they cannot stop thinking of their Guru. For they know that Baba is with them dancing in joy, fulfilling each one's wish and showering them with love.

Baba Hiral Shah was never troubled even in the most difficult of times. On one occasion as Baba danced with joy, I had to give him a disturbing news. Baba heard the news, smiled and danced with joy, while my eyes brimmed with tears. Even on hearing the worrying news, he looked at me and said, 'Don't cry, be happy. Leave your worries to the Almighty.' Baba was not bound to time and knew the future. He was indifferent even to the criticism that came his way.

Baba taught his followers to do good deeds every day and they continue doing so by removing a share from their profits and helping those in need. Baba fed animals and birds daily and helped those in need, he did all he could without making too much noise about it. Till today the needy are provided meals everyday at the temple in Mumbai.

Not many are aware of the relation our Baba shared with Sai Baba even while he was alive. Their relation is that of brothers, guru and disciple and friends. It was his Guru Baba Ashraf Khan who introduced Baba Hiral Shah to Sai Baba. And since that day Baba Hiral Shah never did anything without first seeking permission from Sai. It was through Baba Hiral that his devotees could see Sai. Both are bonded by the common strength, the strength of Almighty and both call out to Allah Malik. Like Sai, Baba Hiral Shah too dedicated his life to the service of mankind. It was Sai Baba's blessings that Baba Hiral Shah took upon himself to open Sai aasthans in as many cities as possible.

In Mumbai, in the Lakshmi Narayan temple, Sai instructed Baba to build a little kutiya (hut) for him. For those who cannot visit Shirdi for any reason, will find solace at the feet of Sai who sits below the Mango tree in the Sai kutiya. Whosoever comes to the kutiya feels the presence of Sai and Baba Hiral Shah. If one visits the kutiya three days consecutively Sai fulfils their wishes. Our Baba Hiral Shah would spend hours at the kutiya and talk to Sai and occasionally dance with joy, a sight that never fades from the memory of his disciples.

Baba Hiral Shah encouraged seekers to do physical service at the aasthans, he said that fortunate are the ones who till their last breath are able to serve Sai. Service can be of any type at an aasthan, cleaning, helping financially or by giving time to the betterment of the aasthans. Singing hymns at aasthans is also a kind of seva as by singing one creates a pious atmosphere. The more prayers are said, the greater the strength of the aasthan.

However, the highest seva in aasthans is handling the shoes of the seekers. A sevadari in charge of handling the seekers footwear receives blessing for his service by Sai. On one occasion a sevadari of the aasthan passed away after completing his shoe seva. Baba Hiral Shah blessed him by keeping the sevadar's head on his lap. Not only was his seva recognised by his guru but also accepted at the doorstep of the Almighty. Blessed are those who have a Guru, who loves them unconditionally.

SAI PARIVAR is blessed by the rarest diamonds, Sai Baba and Baba Hiral Shah.

Miracles of Sai Baba and Baba Hiral Shah

Stop Lying

A follower by the name of Kirti came to Baba. She had been suffering from a severe health issue for a while and finally unable to bear her suffering she visited Baba.

She stood in the queue awaiting her turn as Baba attended to other seekers.

When it was her turn she sat in front of Baba, fell at his feet and wept.

She told Baba about her persisting pain and the incapability of the doctors in finding a solution to her pain. Baba told her that she would be fine only if she made a promise.

Kirti was ready to promise anything, to be cured of her pain. Baba asked her if she was sure and Kirti responded in the positive.

'You have to stop lying Kirti,' Baba commanded.

Kirti was taken aback by Baba's words. It was difficult for her to accept her flaw and she became defensive. Despite being a follower and praying daily she was not ready to accept her Guru's criticism.

Kirti argued with Baba and told him that he was making a mistake. She was not ready to accept that she lied, so how could she promise that she wouldn't lie.

Baba asked her to come back to him after introspecting for a few days. Kirti left disheartened and upset with her Guru.

Two days later Kirti returned to the temple and fell at Baba's feet. In those two days of introspection it struck Kirti that Baba was right. Kirti had been lying about her age to all and believed that it was no big deal lying. She told Baba that she had not realized that this small lie was disrupting her health.

Baba blessed Kirti and explained to her that a lie is a lie whether it is about age or anything else, for it will be added to one's karmic account and that she should promise not to ever lie again.

Seeking forgiveness Kirti promised never to lie again. Within a few days her pain had vanished and Kirti learnt an important lesson.

MORAL: The laws of karma are very stringent and one has to be careful of every thought, word and action.

Baba's love for his disciples

Baba Hiral Shah met every devotee of his with love and treated all his disciples equally.

A family that was completely devoted to Baba were happy that Baba had decided to open an aasthan in their city. With great reverence they bowed to Baba and asked him to give them the opportunity to serve in the aasthan. They wanted liberation and they knew that if they got an opportunity to serve at the aasthan, it would benefit them in every way.

Baba listened to their plea and agreed that they serve at the new aasthan. But Baba knew something was bothering the couple and he asked them about it. At first the couple did not say anything but after Baba's coaxing they spoke of their concern of reaching early morning at the aasthan for Sai seva. Their home was far from the aasthan.

Baba blessed them and told them that Sai would take care. After a few weeks they were elated to know that Baba had arranged for a house near the Sai aasthan. The family was grateful to Baba, for now they would save time and be able to spend more time with their Sai in the aasthan.

Baba wanted his devotees to serve Sai and seek his blessings. Blessings that would help them cut off their past karmas.

On one instance Baba Hiral Shah made arrangement for a car and driver for his disciple who could not commute by himself due to health issues. The disciple was sent a car and driver everyday till he left for his heavenly abode.

Such was the love of Baba towards his disciples.

MORAL: In serving Sai you are helping yourself. Don't ever bloat with pride if you are given a responsibility by Him. Instead bow in humility and be kind to all.

Duty first

Baba always guided his disciples in complying with their duties. Whether as an employer or a boss, a husband or a wife.

Baba explained his disciples that their life was like an umbrella. If even one panel of the umbrella was damaged it would not be able to protect the person from rain. Each panel of the umbrella, depicts a role that we play and the responsibilities we are required to fulfil. As important as it is to give time to family, it is equally necessary to give time to prayers. He also said that it was important to work and connect with loved ones.

He guided his disciples to fulfil all their duties and responsibilities that they have been entrusted with. If a disciple is entrusted with the responsibility of looking after an aasthan, it does not mean that they should forget about their duties towards their family. A balanced life is essential.

On one instance one of Baba's disciples by the name of Jayshree came to the temple to meet Baba. Jayshree was recently married and was a devout follower of Baba. Jayshree was keen on seeing her Guru and disregarded her duties towards her home and went to visit him.

Baba who was attending to the seekers and healing them was surprised to see Jayshree and called for her. Jayshree who was awaiting to meet Baba was questioned by Baba what she was doing at the aasthan when she should have been home attending to the guests.

'Go back and attend to your guests, do your duty first,' Baba instructed Jayshree.

Jayshree was surprised how Baba knew that her mother-in-law was upset with her for ignoring her duties. But Baba knew everything and he always asked his disciples to first comply with their duties at home and then visit Him.

MORAL: Always comply with your duties. Be responsible in life and respect your elders.

Go back

Rani, a devout follower of Sai, visited Baba Hiral Shah to inform him that she was leaving for Shirdi. Baba was told by Sai that Rani had disobeyed her family's wishes and that she should bow at the Sai kutiya for now and not come to Shirdi.

When Baba conveyed Sai's message to Rani, she argued with Baba and said that she had already made the arrangements and would have to go.

Baba Hiral Shah reminded her that she was disobeying Sai's command. But Rani instead of listening to her Guru was adamant to visit Shirdi.

On reaching Shirdi, Rani went to the Samdhi Mandir for darshan. She stood in front of Sai Baba and bowed to Him. Sai Baba asked her get out at that instant and told her that she had not only humiliated him but her Guru too.

Sai's voice was so loud and clear that Rani burst out crying. She apologized to Sai and immediately left for Mumbai.

On reaching Mumbai she fell at her Guru's feet and asked for forgiveness. She was told by Baba Hiral Shah to visit the Sai kutiya for three days. On the third day she heard the voice of Sai commanding her to never ever disregard Baba Hiral Shah ever again.

Rani learnt her lesson and never visited Shirdi till Baba gave her permission to do so.

MORAL: Never disobey your Guru.

Baba's refusal to Sarojini's choice

Baba helped everyone, even if he knew they criticised him behind his back. There were some who would fall at his feet for material gains and once their wish was granted they would turn around and make fun of him and deny the fact that whatever they had received was because of Baba's blessings.

Sarojini loved Baba dearly and went to Baba for his blessings. Sarojini told Baba about her love for her dance instructor. She wanted Baba to convince her parents to let her marry Tarun, the boy she loved.

Baba listened to Sarojini and after meditating he told her that this boy was a wrong choice and she should stay away from him. Sarojini pleaded to Baba to do something because she loved him dearly. But Baba was that if she did marry him, he would use her and leave her.

Blinded by love, Sarojini was upset with Baba for doubting her boyfriend's intention. She trusted her dance teacher more than her Guru.

She disobeyed Baba and married her boyfriend Tarun and as Baba had predicted he lived with her for a few months and then left her for another woman.

Sarojini realized her foolishness and felt ashamed. But her ego would not let her ask for forgiveness from her Guru.

MORAL: No one should under estimate the divine powers of the Guru. If you ask guidance from your Guru, then follow it. Don't be convenient.

Chirag survives

Chirag a dear disciple of Baba Hiral Shah attended every chownki that was held on Thursday's at the Lakshmi Narayan Temple.

In one of the chownkis, Chirag collapsed and fell on the floor. Fortunately, Baba Hiral Shah was present at the temple and the followers immediately took him to Baba's prayer room.

A disciple who was a doctor entered the room to check Chirag's pulse. After checking the pulse, the doctor declared that Chirag was no more. Baba refused to accept the doctor's declaration.

The doctor thought that Baba was in shock and was not accepting the truth. But Baba Hiral Shah insisted that Chirag was alive and kept Chirag's head on His lap and meditated for a while. Baba applied udi on Chirag's forehead and chanted for a while.

The doctor stood confused. He was sure that Chirag was not alive but was amazed to see Baba's faith. After a while Chirag moved his hands and opened his eyes.

Seeing his Guru holding him in his lap, Chirag sat up and bowed to his Guru. He then asked Baba what had happened and why he was sitting in Baba's prayer room?

When Baba told him what had transpired, Chirag was shocked as could not remember anything.

MORAL: If Sai wishes He can bring back the dead.

You are what you eat

Cruelty on animals was something Baba was against and for this reason he asked his followers to convert to vegetarianism. Some disciples followed his command and gave up on consuming non-vegetarian food while there were other disciples who argued with him. Not everyone wanted to change their lifestyle. Especially those that enjoyed dining out felt that in foreign countries choices for vegetarian food were limited.

One such disciple who was a doctor argued with Baba and informed him that it was medically proven that eggs and fish were important for a healthy body.

Baba questioned the professional that why is it that when a human being dies, the arrangements of his final rites are performed immediately?

The doctor replied to Baba that a dead body attracts bacteria, thus it is vital to cremate the body as early as possible.

Baba then asked him, 'is getting a dead animal home and storing it in the freezer healthy?'

The doctor stood silent as he had no answer.

Baba then lovingly explained to his disciple doctor that souls come to Earth to attain salvation, to reunite with the Almighty. Salvation can be attained when one cleanses the soul of the sins that it has accumulated.

'Would you like to stay in a cremation ground?' Baba then questioned the doctor who immediately responded with a 'No.'

'Then how do you expect to be united with the Almighty if your body is a graveyard?' Baba questioned, 'There are energies, vibrations and auras around us that affect our moods. Is that correct?'

The doctor responded in the positive.

'The animal goes through trauma seconds before his death and that trauma lingers on. When humans consume that animal that has been inflicted with pain, they are also ingesting the fear that the animal has experienced.'

The doctor realized his mistake and understood that we are not just our body. We are souls in this body. He apologized to Baba for not understanding the importance of spiritual knowledge.

'You call me your guru then how can you doubt your guru's command. Isn't the guru disciple relation based on trust?' asked Baba.

MORAL: Obedience and acceptance of the guru's command, is an important lesson for every disciple. It is your ego that comes in between you and your guru.

Guru is a shield

Seekers should understand that their Guru is a shield who protects them from negative forces. When a guru gives any instruction, it is important that the disciples follows.

One of Baba's disciple Kalavanti visited Baba and was told by Baba that she had weak legs.

Kalavanti asked Baba to help her and Baba asked her to order a silver anklet for her left leg. Kalavanti followed her Baba's instruction and got a silver anklet made to her size and brought it to Baba.

Baba blessed the anklet and asked Kalavanti to wear it and never ever remove it in her life.

As years passed by Kalavanti forgot about Baba's instruction and removed the silver anklet and kept it aside. Kalavanti moved around without the anklet that Baba had blessed to protect her from negative attacks.

After two months of moving around without the anklet, Kalavanti had a fall and had to undergo three surgeries on her ankle. Unaware that she had disobeyed her Guru's command she cried out to Baba for help as she was unable to bear the pain.

Kalavanti heard the voice of her Baba Hiral Shah, 'Didn't I tell you never to remove the anklet, then why did you?'

Kalavanti realized her mistake of not following her Guru's command. She had completely forgotten of the promise she had made to Baba. Till she had the anklet on her weak legs were protected by the silver anklet that had acted as a shield.

MORAL: Don't underestimate the power of your guru's words. A guru can foresee your future and warns you accordingly and if you don't follow his command you have to bear the consequences. It is important to listen to your guru. His blessings act as a shield from negativity

Humility

Children born into rich families are pampered and not aware of the harsh realities of life. When they leave their parents abode, they are unable to face the truth.

Baba always guided his disciples to instil good values in their children. He would always say that parents should lead by example. Not all parents were capable of controlling their children and they would then go to Baba for guidance.

Most of the disciple's children enjoyed Baba's company for he would talk to them as a friend and teach them important lessons of life. They would then share their issues with Baba who would guide them to the right path.

One such girl Padma, whose parents were devout followers pleaded Baba to guide their daughter. Padma was brought up in luxury and comfort. As she grew older and was ready for marriage her parents worried about her capability to run her home.

Padma's parents went to Baba and pleaded for guidance as they could not handle their daughter. They were worried about her future. Baba asked them to leave their daughter under his and his wife's vigilance. The parents accepted Baba's offer and left Padma in their Guru's home. Padma loved her Baba and as per his command took training under Baba's wife and learnt to run a home and became a very good cook. Baba made sure that Padma was not only good at running a home but also would be capable of running a business. He trained her in finance management too.

Within a year Padma had transformed from a spoilt girl to an intelligent and humble woman. Her parents were grateful to Baba and within a few months Padma was married to a gentleman from Africa.

Padma missed her guru in Africa. She prayed to Baba that she and her family should shift to India so she can be close to him and the aasthan. Baba fulfilled her wish and Padma moved to India along with her husband and children. Her dream of doing seva at the aasthans was fulfilled.

MORAL: It is important for parents to instil good values in their children. Lead by example. Inculcating good habits and discipline in children at a young age will make them responsible adults.

Baba blesses Tara and Mohan with a child

Tara and Mohan were married for many years but could not conceive a child. They visited many doctors and underwent treatments but nothing helped.

When Tara and Mohan heard about Baba from a friend, they decided to visit India and seek his blessings.

They prayed to Baba to bless them with a child. The ever-merciful Baba asked the couple to pray to Lord Nandlala (Baby Krishna) in the Lakshmi Narayan Temple for eleven days.

Tara and Mohan followed Baba's instruction and religiously visited the temple every morning and prayed to Nandlala.

After eleven days of prayers, they bowed at Baba's feet. Baba blessed the couple and told them that their prayers would soon be answered. The couple was joyous on hearing Baba's words and flew back to their home in States.

As Baba had predicted, within three months Tara found out that she was pregnant. Where doctors had failed, prayers had worked. With Nandlala and Baba's blessings they were blessed with a son.

Just like Tara and Mohan many couples had been blessed by Baba. And even today whosoever visits Sai kutiya for eleven days and reads the Sai dhuni finds their wishes being fulfilled. Baba Hiral Shah may have left his mortal body, but his presence is felt in Sai aasthans all over the world.

Devotees who love Baba with a pure heart can feel his presence everywhere and at times they can see him physically. One such incident happened when a disciple unaware of Baba's death reached the aasthan bowed in front of the chair that Baba sat on. Baba sat there physically and conversed with him. When he stepped out and was told about Baba's death he was stunned. Those disciples who truly love Baba see him today also in the aasthan.

One time, when one of Baba's disciples asked Baba the path to liberation, Baba responded that service to Sai is higher than liberation. Pray to Sai that whenever he needs someone to fulfil any purpose on this earth, that he chooses you. A lesson that is inscribed in the hearts of his followers.

'Your birth is justified if you manage to put it to use towards betterment of humanity.'

Baba Hiral Shah

MORAL: Those who visit the aasthans with full faith will find their wishes being fulfilled. Spend your time in service of humanity.

Thank you SAI for your guidance,
Thank you SAI for your love,
Thank you SAI for your blessings,
Thank you SAI for your kind words,
At your feet I lay your work.

Please bless it and let it be read and heard,
Om Sai Ram.
Sai Hira Ram.

Printed in Great Britain
by Amazon